Serbian born Mladen Jakovljevic travelled around the globe while working on cruise ships for ten years. Driven by his enthusiastic and adventurous spirit, Mladen never stopped seeking justice and fighting for fair and equal treatment of all people, particularly employees in lower-ranked positions in big companies.

Thank you to all the seamen worldwide, warriors of the sea, and people who sacrifice the present moment to create a better future for their families. Indeed, you are the real brave heroes of the seven seas. You are working long, exhausting hours for a seven-day straight for 7–10 months without a day off; with unfair working conditions and a slavery management regime, it's not easy. Yet, you have chosen to keep your smile on, push every obstacle along the way, and make a better life for your families back home. I truly admire all of you!

Mladen Jakovljevic

Modern Age Slavery

Austin Macauley Publishers™
London • Cambridge • New York • Sharjah

All of the events in this memoir are true to the best of author's memory. The views expressed in this memoir are solely those of the author.

A CIP catalogue record for this title is available from the British Library.

ISBN 9781398492394 (Paperback)
ISBN 9781398492400 (Hardback)
ISBN 9781398492424 (ePub e-book)
ISBN 9781398492417 (Audiobook)

www.austinmacauley.com

First Published 2022
Austin Macauley Publishers Ltd®
1 Canada Square
Canary Wharf
London
E14 5AA

I want to give my sincere gratitude to Austin Macauley Publishers for believing in me from the very beginning. This fantastic company offered me phenomenal support throughout the book publishing process. It's easy to believe in people who have already reached certain status and level of fame. Yet, your fantastic company is unique in a fabulous way; you collaborated your professional services and unconditionally inspired first-time unknown publishers to accomplish their dreams. You are a beautiful example that there is hope in this world. Austin Macauley Publishers represents the voice of justice for millions of people around the globe. Indeed, a spectacular kind of support, professionalism. I would like to acknowledge and recognize all the people who supported me on my journey. For every seaman, a journey at sea is usually a daily battle with loneliness. Thank you to my family, who always stood up behind me and supported me, especially during the ten years of working on the cruise ship. Furthermore, thank you to all of my respected guests who made a tremendous difference for my entire family. The smallest gesture of kindness from my lovely guests gave me enormous energy to remain strong, dedicated to my goal of providing a better future for my family back home.

Introduction:
Behind the Scenes

This book is based on a true story. It should provide you with a clear picture of what it takes to work on a cruise ship; it emphasises the enormous sacrifice from seamen worldwide. While working onboard the cruise ship for ten years, many of my respectful guests asked me questions about what it looks like to live and work on the cruise ship. In fact, for our passengers on board, we had something called 'Behind the scenes tour' where our guests would be taken on a four-hour tour so they would be able to see some of the crew facilities on board. During that tour, a guest could have a little taste of how the crew life on board looks like, and they could explore the crew areas, crew mess, engine control room, crew bar. It also cost our guest 110 dollars to do that, and yet, there were limited spots for that particular ship tour due to high demand, often it was booked out in a few hours.

'Modern age slavery' is my 'Behind the scenes tour' for all people who wanted to know more about the reality of the crew members' life on board the cruise ship. It should primarily serve as a voice of justice and shout out to millions of hard-working crew members worldwide. They sacrifice a moment of presence to create a better future for their families.

By presenting particular events from the time when I was a crew member on board the biggest cruise line company globally, my idea was to highlight all irregularities and unfair treatment that crew members on the cruise ships are exposed to every day. After reading this book, you will gain a different perspective on the cruising industry. You will be able to understand what is behind those glorious, sensational passengers' views from their balcony cabins, what occurred behind the regular crew member's curtain on board.

Therefore, while writing this book, my greatest dream and inspiration was to influence future sailors to have a more compassionate approach for the crew members. I also desired to help people who have decided to work on the cruise ship with important but realistic information about a seaman's life. More importantly, my biggest motivation was to possibly create new rules and regulations for all the seaman to be implemented fair, equal treatment, and better management onboard the cruise ships.

Moreover, an incident happened onboard the cruise ship; I was injured while performing my daily task in one of the ship's bars. Instead of providing me with much-needed medical assistance and support at that time, the cruise line company distanced from this incident and let me suffer on my own. They even ordered a cover-up of that particular incident on board. They refused to help me anyhow in my complicated recovering stage, sending me away from the cruise ship without proper medical treatment and therapy.

Unfortunately, the cruise ship industry is almost untouchable regarding their illegal actions against the crew members. Liability does not exist because cruise lines register their ships in Panama, Bahamas, Vanuatu, etc. It operates under the flag state law and usually has lesser regulations and labour policies. This harms its crew because the company does not need to comply with US maritime law. For that reason, malpractices on board the cruise ships often go unnoticed and kept being hidden underneath. Deficient standards of working conditions exist, just like in a slavery regime. I genuinely hope that this book will create some positive difference for millions of workers worldwide.

Chapter 1
Journey, Not a Destination

The flight from Atlanta to Miami was delayed for a couple of hours. Tired and lonely, finally I have got on the plane. Unexpectedly, I sat down on my seat next to the two FBI agents and two Mexican prisoners who were probably transferred to another jail in Florida. I held a small prayer book and my wife and kid's pictures in my sweaty hand. Another eight-month contract onboard the ship in front of me, I thought about it unintentionally – it will take forever until I see my family again. While I was observing two handcuffed Mexican prisoners next to me, I realised that, just for my freedom, I was a rich man. I have a beautiful family waiting for me to return home after completing my eight-month contract onboard the cruise ship. Once again, I will have an opportunity to visit numerous tourist destinations, meet many great people, and expand my knowledge in various life areas. Therefore, life was beautiful, or maybe I just wanted to bombard myself with positive thoughts to prevent sadness caused by separation anxiety. Probably, after ten years of working onboard the cruise ships, somehow, I have learned to trick myself into a good mood in those moments when I felt down.

The plane landed in Miami. The new contract, new challenges were waiting for me. But I was ready. Work pressure is okay; I thought so. We never know what we are truly capable of until we are being pushed to do it.

While disembarking the plane at Miami airport, I felt a new dose of positivity in my veins. I can do it. For my family, I will make them proud.

Drained and physically exhausted after several connecting flights from my home country to the US, I was on the edge of physical energy. After the plane landed, my goal was to quickly find my luggage and get on the transfer bus to a hotel where the company booked my stay for the night. It was already 8 pm. Ideally, I planned to arrive at the hotel around 9 pm to grab some dinner and rest, but it was not as smooth as expected. In the baggage pick-up area at Miami international airport, I found out that my luggage was lost somewhere on the way. That would not be a huge issue if I was not a crew member on the cruise ship. In ten years of working on the cruise ship, I have learned the same lesson; we cannot control all events and things around us, yet, we can, and we should always control how we react to it. I was trying to remain calm. Slowly, I walked into an office for lost luggage and filled up the form. They explained that there is a probability that luggage could arrive in Miami the following day and be sent directly to my hotel before joining the ship. Indeed, it was a complicated and an uncertain scenario. Because the very next day, I was about to enter the vessel for the new eight months contract, and without my luggage, it would be nearly impossible. What if luggage does not arrive on time, and all of my essential personal belongings?

Finally, around 11 pm, I have arrived at the hotel. Loud and friendly shuttle driver Claudio from Colombia wished me a bit of good luck upon arrival. The friendly staff at the front desk also made me feel welcome; they gave me a breakfast voucher for the following day and ensured that they would do whatever it took to help me with my lost luggage. The hotel staff provided me with a temporary shaving kit and a small toothbrush to refresh myself after a long connecting flight. The spacious, beautiful hotel room provided me with an opportunity to rest before joining the ship. Complimentary room service, the comfortable king-size bed, I felt like a one-million-dollar man at that moment. For sure, if I was not already an experienced sea wolf, I would probably get tricked by this modern, cosy hotel comfort for a moment. But I knew something else, for a fact, the upcoming day would bring less sweet reality, and that was true, indeed.

After a few hours of much-needed rest, I woke up with a great news, my luggage was found and delivered in the hotel lobby. Sufficient to say that made a huge difference. Being again in possession of my personal belongings gave me a sense of security and peace of mind. A polite staff member at the front desk and proper breakfast rounded up my extraordinary hotel experience. That morning I was about to leave my comfort zone again for the next eight months. Inevitable challenges lay ahead of me, but I was mentally prepared for adversity onboard the cruise ship.

While waiting for the shuttle bus, I encountered some deep thoughts. Almost ten years ago, I came to work on the cruise ship for the first time, and the night before joining my first ship, I stayed in this same hotel. I had $5 in my pocket when I arrived, and I was eager and determined to make it happen. Young boy at that time, brave but not smart enough. At that time, I wanted to come to work on a cruise ship to buy a super-fast car, a big house, and a fancy motorcycle. I thought that something 'over there' would equate to the finishing line in our life, which I need to accomplish to be happy in this world. It took me nearly ten years to learn that happiness cannot be achieved by our imaginary material goals. Because even if we do so, that would just become an endless circle of our new expectations. When we reached out to a specific purpose, we immediately set another one. And another one. It never ends. We often waste our lifetime, focusing only on our future goals and sacrificing the present moment's beauty. I was standing in the same hotel many years later and observing myself in front of the mirror while waiting for the bus to take me to the ship again.

I have concluded that I am a happy man, even though I still did not achieve my dreams from ten years ago. Simply, I have stopped running around and trying to reach any of those tangible goals. Suddenly, I realised that I no longer needed a fast car or a big fancy house. While traveling around the world, I have found a sense of inner peace and joy in helping others whenever possible. Meanwhile, I have met my beautiful wife, my most significant support and inspiration. I became a father of two wonderful boys. I have also met some fantastic people on board the cruise ships, colleagues, managers, and leaders, unbelievable people who taught me a lot about the real value. Honestly, I was sincerely thankful for all those people because they helped me find my purpose, and they all became my greatest asset in this world.

Suddenly, while waiting for the shuttle bus to take me to the cruise ship terminal, I realised that life is a journey, not a destination. And yet, I was thankful for the unforgettable journey up to that moment.

The bus arrived in front of the hotel, and it was time for a new adventurous departure in the mystery of the blue ocean. Accumulated cruise ship experience at that moment helped me to remain calm and to focus on the upcoming challenges. Maturity and years of cruise ship experience calm me before a massive storm.

Knowing all of that, I had started taking slow, uncertain steps towards the shuttle bus. While putting my baggage on the bus, I heard a beautiful bird chirp on nearby trees. It was a sunny, bright, and good morning that made me feel that I can have enough strength and energy to complete one more contract. While the bus was on the way to the port terminal, I observed the other 50 crew members' anxious faces. Some of them were first time joining the cruise ship as crew members. They were separated from their families for the first time to provide a better future for their loved ones.

On top of their inner insecurity, they wore one fake, sour smile on their faces. But that smiles already meant something, determination, courage; those crew members were brave enough to explore an unknown sea journey on their own, far away from their countries and families.

My genuine, unsolicited advice to all of them was to take one day at a time and believe that they need to get out of their comfort zone for them to grow (Maxwell, 1993). After four hours of drive from Miami to Port Canaveral, we finally arrived at the cruise ship terminal, ready to sign on and prepared to overcome our fears and push our limits to some new, undiscovered heights. A new journey was about to begin.

Chapter 2
Embarkation

Upon arrival at the cruise ship terminal, I have instantly noticed that crew members around me looked more and more anxious. It was an apparent fear on their faces; even they were trying hard to cover up with a huge fake smile on their faces. We got off the bus quickly, almost in an orderly manner, all of us lined up in front of the crew members' port terminal. It was not long after the HR coordinator counted all present crew members and ensured everyone got their required documents. Shortly after, in the small, isolated corner of the cruise ship terminal, we were left for another hour, standing on the sun's heat.

At 11:30 am, some loud noises occasionally broke the silence between the joining crew from thousands of the guests near the passenger terminal, ready to board the vessel. That was such a striking difference. Crew members, who looked like they were about to be shot, drained, and most of them were exhausted from the long flights, waiting on the Florida sun's heat for their chance to shine. They needed to impress and comply with company management's demands on board – saving the last drops of energy to stand on their feet. On the other side, just nearby on the passenger terminal, happy, excited guests loudly danced their way into the majestic cruise experience.

There is a massive misconception about the veteran crew member's ship's status. Mistakenly, many people believed that experienced crew members got used to being away from their families after several years of working on cruise ships. How wrong? It only gets harder instead of getting used to it after years of service onboard the cruise ship. That is why we often hear the sentence from the older crew members, "This is my last contract." I felt the same way on that day. No matter how many contracts I have already completed, it only gets harder and harder every time I come back to join the ship. The reason behind; time is inevitably passing by for all of us. Along the way, we learn that there is no pause button where we could somehow 'freeze the time' and achieve all of our material goals and then press the button again and start enjoying life. In the life master lesson, we learned that material things are not paid for with money; we get paid with time spent away from our family (Covey, 1989).

It was almost 1 pm when we finally got on board the cruise ship. Security screening, endless documents, and tons of new information are just like icing on the cake for newly joined crew members. That is usually the most challenging moment of the entire contract of each individual. Our orientation program was scheduled at 2 pm. I could see confusion from all the information given for newly signed crew members pretending that they were on the top of the game.

After the onboard safety presentations, we had meeting with department managers, received our working schedules, and heard more about company expectations, rules, and regulations. They also gave us safety vests and emergency cards. When the general safety briefing for guests and crew finished around 4 pm, it was time to find our cabins, one of the most critical and exciting factors for crew members on board, simply because they will be sharing a 7 square metre cabin. The cabin felt like a shoebox for someone like me, especially with a random roommate from some of the 72 different nationalities on board.

Chapter 3
Crew Members' Lives Matter

That day I got lucky. I met my new cabin mate, Gabor. He looked neat and clean, which is a big deal when sharing a small cabin with someone. As we walked around and still felt lost in the crew area searching for our place, we finally found cabin number B442. It was located two decks below level zero. I was dragging my baggage through the tinny metal stairs to get surprised when I saw the red tape right in front of our cabin. Gabor was staring at me, confused for a moment. Still, I calmly explained that the housekeeping department probably cleaned the crew corridor and marked the area in front of our cabin with red tape to avoid passing.

Gently, I removed the tape in front of the door as we entered the small place for the first time. I knew everything was shocking for Gabor, Hungarian assistant waiter, who was stepping on the cruise ship for the first time, so I took extra time to guide him through all the necessary details about life on board. He seemed like a nice guy, polite and friendly. When we entered our cabin, it was 4 pm.

I was expected to show up at work precisely at 5 pm, and no matter how many times I have come to a crew cabin, it still felt shocking. It was weird on top of everything because of some unusual details that we came across.

The upper bed was still not fixed and tidied up, with remaining old linen from the previous crew member before we came. That was quite strange because housekeeping would always properly place clean beddings for all newly signed crew members. Also, we have found shoes and a cook's uniform in the small shoe rack underneath the bed cabinet. Gabor could hardly speak English; therefore, it was hard for us to communicate. Despite that language barrier, I tried to help him adjust to a new living and working environment. He pointed at wrinkled clothes on the small cabinet, and probably he was bothered by it as much as I was. Surprises kept coming as we have found more personal belongings from someone else. I have found a letter and a name tag of an Indian cook on the upper bunk bed under the pillowcase. It was getting more confusing; why would the crew coordinator let us enter the cabin not appropriately cleaned, and more importantly – what was this red tape in front of our cabin door?

Gabor was only at his first contract on the cruise ship, and for him, this was way too much to handle. Quickly, I went upstairs in the Linen Room to get new clean linen and some pillowcases. Every cruise ship has a different class and size, and upon our arrival, it can take about two weeks to learn all crew and guest corridors on board. The linen room for the crew members was on Deck C, one level down our cabin, and so I went there, took clean linen, blankets, pillowcases, fresh towels for both of us, which the housekeeping department usually does.

Gabor seemed to be physically and emotionally drained with sorrow in his eyes after long flights from the day before, information overflowing upon getting on board and the top, all this mystery with red tape around our small cabin. Being a somehow experienced crew member, I have tried to calm him down and to encourage him that everything will be okay. "Gabor, I know this might seem like a little too much to handle at this moment. Every beginning is hard; that is normal. In the long run, these challenges will certainly make you feel stronger, and all this will become a valuable experience for your future; take one day at a time, I will help you with everything as much as I can."

He did not show any reaction to my words. His eyes, tears were pouring down like sudden rain. We both needed to get ready for our first day at work onboard the cruise ship, yet it seemed that Gabor was not prepared to take on these challenges. It is not a health-friendly environment far from our families, stuck in the smallest cabin globally. I have learned how to deal with that and suppress my feelings throughout my career. But with Gabor, I could sense that he was anxious and homesick.

Instinctively, I decided to give him some privacy and time. Quickly I left the cabin and ran upstairs to the crew coordinator's office. I was trying to get more information about that red tape in our cabin. A long line of newly signed crew members who were waiting in front of the crew office. When my turn came up, I politely approached the crew office desk, and I showed them the plastic bag where I gathered all the stuff of that Indian cook. "Excuse me, madam, maybe you can help me understand why we were given a cabin that is still occupied, or if not, then is it maybe the housekeeping in charge forgot or missed to clean our cabin? I have found clothes, a cook's uniform, one can of soda, shoes, and some letters I assumed in the Indian language. Also, do you know anything about the red tape wrapped around our room?"

"Is that cabin B422?" she asked me loudly. The crew coordinator looked like she knew something but not willing to share the information with me.

Finally, with a hesitation in her voice, she said, "Okay, listen… A crew member went missing on our last voyage three days ago. The Captain and Staff Captain have ordered a full investigation of that case, and therefore, the housekeeping department could not fully prepare that cabin for your arrival. Police were on board this morning before you guys signed on the ship, and an investigation is still ongoing."

I interrupted her in disbelief, saying, "I am confused why we were assigned to that cabin with all the personal belongings from that person who probably went overboard three days ago?"

I immediately asked if they could move us to another cabin. The crew coordinator seemed to be not bothered or concerned at all. She said, "There is no other available cabin on board at this time. I am afraid you do not choose to stay in that cabin until they find a newly available crew cabin."

Blood rushed through my brain, and I became so uneasy. However, I had to keep my composure as I was getting ready for my first working day.

An Indian crew member went missing; I heard some information before that incident; he complained to his colleagues that he was fed up with how the management dealt with him in inhumane working conditions. Days after, he went missing, and according to the police investigation, he jumped overboard, based on the ship's CCTV. He also wrote a letter to his family, which is the same letter I found under the pillow.

This whole scenario has had a chilling effect on my roommate, me, and the entire crew. Most of us crew members wondered, and there were so many unanswered questions going through our heads. I could not help but think that the Human Resource should be on top of this situation, especially in assisting and supporting the crew members cope with the recent event. The management ordered a meeting right after they released the information about the investigation. According to management, the missing crew member had 'many personal problems at home'.

I am trying hard to believe in that reasoning, but it is not about that. I have witnessed and experienced the same thing as that missing crew member. I always think that the crew members were just a number and could be easily replaced, which was confirmed with this case. Unofficially, later on, I found out from several other crew members that the missing crew member was exposed to inadequate treatment; he was always yelled at and threatened to be fired. I think that he probably could not handle the pressure from his supervisors anymore and felt helpless.

Financial goals and targets were the priorities on board, and there was no space for empathy and compassion towards crew members. The management team would often say to us, "If you do not like working here, go home, there are millions of people waiting for your job." Sarcastically, how encouraging and motivating that sounds. As I always try to look on the other side of the coin and keep a positive perspective, I can't still help but think that the company is not providing enough regulations, policies, and services to ensure its crew's well-being. That company has failed in maintaining a healthy working environment.

Chapter 4
Difficulty in adjusting

Life onboard the cruise ships also has a lot of benefits indeed. Around 1500 crew members on board, simultaneously working like a Swiss clock, provide a memorable experience for our guests. There is no such working environment elsewhere where you can see so many smiley faces around. A variety of backgrounds and cultural beliefs, 72 different nationalities onboard the cruise ship, yet everyone seems happy and dedicated to providing a better life to their families back home. My job as a bartender sounds simple, a three-step job. Make drinks, put a massive smile on your face, provide a quality service to the guest. Yet, it is not that simple, and that is for sure.

Upon joining the vessel, the first week onboard is packed with safety meetings and trainings, it is completely overwhelming for any crew member trying to adjust to ship life. Even for the experienced seaman, it can be way too stressful. Our working hours were different depending on if it was a sea day or port day. Frankly speaking, sea day felt like it's never-ending.

I have to get up around 7 am for a wellness check-in at the ship's medical centre. After that, all newly signed crew had to complete four hours of safety training. The training finished somewhere around 11:30 am, just in time to grab a quick lunch before work. The official working schedule for me started at noontime.

As an 'experienced' bartender, I was allocated in one of the busiest bars onboard, either a Casino bar on Deck 5 or a Pool bar on Deck 10. Every contract is a new beginning because we all have new colleagues, supervisors, and managers; it usually takes weeks to adjust.

My dinner break was at 5 pm, and then work continued from 7 pm until 3 am the next day, with a few short breaks in between. The average working hours on sea days are 12 hours. That probably would not be an issue if work ends there. Living on board the ship includes other responsibilities besides the job itself. I had to do my laundry around 4 am and wash and iron my clothes and uniform. It was impossible to do that during the day because we had 1500 crew members onboard the ship, and there were only ten laundry machines, far below what was realistically required. My work would finish very late, and it was the only chance to spend another two hours and complete this necessary task. Around 6 am, deep into the following morning, when most crew members from different departments were about to start a new day at work, it was finally my time to rest after 24 hours of an eventful and demanding day.

The solid military discipline that I have enforced on myself gave me a sense of purpose and security. Carefully, I have opened a heavy metal door of my cabin. It was around 6:30 am. I have learned the importance of care and respect towards others throughout the cruise ships. Especially when you share the smallest cabin in the world with someone else, mutual respect is much needed and appreciated. I slowly opened a small cabinet to put my clothes and uniform away. The goal was to have at least two hours of sleep before the mandatory general safety drill scheduled that morning upon arriving at our first port, Montego Bay, Jamaica.

Suddenly, around 7 am my roommate started to shout very loud, "Mum… Help me!" At first, I slowly moved my curtain and observed the unexpected situation in front of my eyes. I was not even sure if Gabor was sleeping or not; his eyes were wide open. He held on to his crouched knees and cried loudly while sitting on the cabin floor. Slowly, I approached him with a comforting voice, "It's okay, buddy, I know it is hard. I promise I will help you out with everything; just let me know."

He looked tired, over drained, and emotionally unstable. There was no response from him; I was unsure if he had some kind of breakdown. It took another one hour to calm him down finally. I sat down on the floor next to him during that time, and I tried my best to encourage him to remain strong.

Adversity on board the cruise ship is inevitable, and each person deals with it uniquely. Finally, Gabor mumbled something unclearly, "I want to go home; I don't feel good here anymore. They make me feel worthless. They treat me like an animal here."

Unfortunately, that was the last day of work for him. He was taken to the shoreside hospital because he had a nervous breakdown. Shortly after, he was sent home.

It made me think about what Gabor told me that morning. Crew members onboard the ship are already separated from their families and friends for seven to nine months. We exposed ourselves to rude, obnoxious passengers, unusual, challenging living conditions, long working hours.

Work on the cruise ship never stops; there are no days off, Sundays, public holidays, or New Year celebrations. On top of that, management is obsessed with the power in their hands, yet often they are untrained or not qualified for their roles. Instead of making crew members' lives a little more comfortable, they go around and whip the crew mercilessly.

Our company created a specific management module that will only focus on draining the crew members' life. When those crew members became out of use, a new replacement was waiting as we had never been there before. That system worked well in the past, and the company was financially growing bigger; new ships were coming out every year.

Like Gabor, many other crew members paid the high price with a permanently damaged health condition, often because of the stress level experienced and the brutal treatment in the hands of unqualified supervisors.

Without a doubt, a lack of authentic leadership could lead to disaster, not only on the cruise ships but in life generally.

Instead of feeling self-pity, I have decided to educate myself and diligently study leadership's importance. I have read books and educated myself accordingly for most of my free time. My dream was to conduct various studies to understand how to change this poor management onboard cruise ships. Therefore, I have decided to do a lot of research, and I gave myself a few months to present my project to the highest company management. That was my idea of change; I was invigorated by it.

After a couple of weeks on board, I finally got the chance to step on the land, and at least for two hours, I got out of this hectic cruise ship environment. I have decided to visit the library in Port Canaveral, Florida. That day, I spent my savings and bought more than 20 books about leadership, written mainly by John Maxwell and Stephen Covey, two of the world's most prominent leadership experts. My goal was to clarify objectives and ways of attaining them precisely. To create a happy working environment, have a fair workplace where every crew member will be well respected, motivated, and inspired to perform consistently at their highest capacity and potential. It should be a win-win environment where everyone wins, the company and its crew members simultaneously. Consequently, that would logically result in better customer service as well.

What a huge goal I had! Problems along the way? Many, I would say. Frankly speaking, my position itself was the first obstacle. I was still just a bartender, taking no part in any management decisions on board. But that was not a decisive factor. My motivation and desire made a difference.

Since day one on board the cruise ship, back in 2008, I was always an outspoken, change-oriented individual who fought for fair and equal treatment of all employees.

Unfortunately, it took me a while to learn the painful lesson – company needed loyal 'dogs' to be part of their brutal slavery manner, people who would be willing to do many unethical things to ensure uphill profit growth.

After ten years, I thought I was ready to create a significant change. I set a very high goal. I have planned to do intensive research, study, and create a new 'Leadership Development Program' for the company. Honestly, I was invigorated by this idea of lasting change. During the first three weeks on board, I have worked hard and studied hard.

My goals were crystal clear, to create a permanent management change that will positively impact the lives of millions of crew members worldwide.

What a bold and ambitious idea!

Chapter 5
Sailing Alone Through the Storm

My new roommate, who replaced Gabor, was from Indonesia. His name was Gede, and he worked as a bar steward, certainly one of the most challenging jobs. Our communication was limited due to intense working hours and different schedules. Gede was collecting the garbage from the 20 bars that he was assigned. His monthly salary was $500, and he worked for around 80 hours per week.

The company had a nasty trick in instructing department managers to cover actual working hours. As part of the company policy, crew members at the start of their day shift were required to 'log in' for duty. After completing our work for the day, the total working hours should never exceed ten hours. However, my roommate Gede told me that he was often instructed to 'clock out' for the day, and after that, he was sent back to complete more jobs. That way, Gede's total working hours would officially in the systems still comply with rules and regulations. One of the many unofficial actions on board the ship was the slavery regime on the next level.

Despite all of that, the approach to my job was always consistent. A huge smile on my face made a lasting impact on our guest experience every single day. Regardless of anything, I took pride in what I do, taking a bartender job to a very professional level. Undoubtedly, there were days when I was feeling flat, when I missed my family too much, yet I still completed all my tasks and performed my duty at the highest level.

Besides that, I was in charge of the bar operation at the busiest bar on board, the pool bar on Deck 10. It is located right next to the pool and jacuzzi and is known to be one of the guests' favourite locations because of the fancy surroundings and the food buffet nearby.

Uncertainty

Sometimes I felt like being on the edge of the cliff. When am I going to see my family again? How could my managers on board the ship be so shallow and unfair? On top of all those concerns, some unpleasant guests were my regular daily challenges. However, no matter how hard it was, I always kept in mind that the darkest hour of the night always comes just before dawn (Maxwell, 2009). I desired to create a lasting legacy for all seamen around the world. That kept me going forward.

My idea was to prompt the change in terms of the working conditions on the cruise ship forever.

Random sea day

Here is an attempt to explain one average working day onboard.

Most of the time, after two hours of sleep, I would wake up in the morning with only one question remaining in my mind, why am I still stuck here. Tired of unrealistically long working hours, I was dragging myself out of bed.

Most of the time, my anticipated working schedule was saying that I should be finished precisely at midnight. Still, because of extra cleaning duties and some public health inspections expecting to board the vessel anytime, we have stayed at work until 4 am. The schedule is one thing on paper; practically, it is something different.

So I guess that explains why I felt drained and over fatigued when I woke up in the morning. Just getting off the bed was a real struggle itself.

The first goal for the morning was simple – try not to hit a shallow cabin ceiling; it seemed like a Special Force training should be required to move around my cabin. A small toilet was shared with another cabin, so it was pretty rare for me to get a chance to use it right away.

Here I am, on the way out of my cabin, but not going to work yet, because my official schedule for the day starts in the afternoon. For now, I will be part of the mandatory safety briefing that is scheduled on my time off work.

Safety briefing took place from 9:30 until 10:30. Finally, it is finished around 10:30 am, and now I am running to my cabin, trying to get at least another one hour of sleep before going to work. When I finally got a chance to stretch my numbing feet on the bed, the phone rang. My manager called me to come to his office immediately because I was scheduled to be part of the medical centre's random alcohol and drug test. Having no alternative option, I went to the security office and the medical centre; it took an hour to get that part done. Now, at this point, there won't be any more time to rest. It's noon, and it's time to go to work.

Consequently, just when I got back to my cabin, I started to feel unwell. I felt dizzy, and some strange pain was going through my left hand.

Going back to the infirmary to get medical advice was my only option. As I entered the medical centre, I politely excused myself and asked if I could maybe see the doctor with a massive smile on my face. In exchange for my friendly approach, the nurse immediately gave me that grumpy look, which I try to interpret as, "Why you are here, I am sure that you are just trying to get a day off from your work?"

Yet, she does not say that because there are plenty of guests sitting in the waiting area, and of course, the nurse is very polite to them. But in my case, from her perspective, I was probably classified as an unimportant human being who was wasting her time and energy, and that was exactly how she looked at me. Finally, after a few minutes of giving me a grumpy look, she said to me, "What do you want?"

At the back of my mind, I was saying to myself, "Oh, hang on. Sorry, I probably have nothing else to do, so I just came here to give you a hard time for nothing."

But I did not say that; I guess I should. My values and behaviour would never be diverted because of some disrespectful person who would try to put me down. No, it won't happen.

With an apparent hesitation and confusion, I finally replied, "I am sorry, maybe you guys are busy with our guest… I might stop by later on."

After spending another hour of my break for nothing, I left the medical centre without being medically assessed. On my way back to work, I struggled physically and mentally. I had a lot of ongoing problems back home at the same time, with so many thoughts going through my head. Yet, my job was to smile and be helpful, and somehow I have mastered performing under pressure. Despite all experienced feelings and being tired, drained in every way that one person can be, I kept smiling and greeted every person who came across my path. I did not allow my problems and feelings to affect my work and people around. Despite all, I tried my best and successfully created a positive difference for thousands of guests that I served that busy day. Why? I decided to act myself into feeling good! It took a lot of effort on the days like this to come out there and become a positive influencer, difference maker, someone who creates memories for our respectful guests. It takes a horrendous effort to get rid of the victim's state of mind.

That is what I was doing on the cruise ship. I have decided not to give up. That day, I have worked for 15 hours straight. After a long and tiring shift, I dragged myself into my tiny cabin. The ship rocked so much, and my baggage moved from the left to right side, hitting the cabin walls.

Just when I was finally about to take a rest after a very long day, the phone rang again. It was my manager. "Please, come straight to the office. I need to see you urgently." I got up from my bed and quickly came to the bar office without further hesitation. It was already almost 4 am. I thought that I could not get any more tired than that, yet I felt that my body was slowly collapsing minute by minute. My feet were swollen, and I could not walk properly. Without saying sorry for disturbing me at this late hour, without any logical excuse, my manager said to me straight, "There was an incident involving a few of our passengers last night. You were the last person who served them an alcoholic beverage, so you will need to make a statement according to company policy. Security officers will come to take you to their office, and all you need to do is write down a short statement about those passengers who were involved in the incident. Don't worry, it will be quick."

I was shocked. It was 4:30 am, and my new day at work was about to start again in only a few hours, yet I was still stuck in the office.

"This is all wrong; with all respect, sir, I was working hard all day long, and I should be off duty a long time ago. How on earth could you possibly expect me to be fresh, efficient, and polite with our guests tomorrow? I did not have a proper sleep already for several days, and I am working 12–15 hour shifts! I felt this doesn't seem right."

I was getting frustrated already. Instead of showing empathy and compassion, the manager replied to me, "This is part of your job. It does not end when you go to your cabin. If you are not happy, there are thousands of people who are ready to take your job. Just let me know, any time."

Wow. What an inspiring manager. Leader? For sure, not. What a lack of emotional intelligence! Instead of trying to find an emphatic answer, he made it even harder for me. I almost felt like collapsing there at the scene, yet my manager showed zero compassion.

While I was walking towards the security office, something struck me like lightning. Why am I still working for this company? If money is my answer, how could I not identify any other income source than this slavery system? I have developed experience at my job throughout the years, and for sure many skills were not utilised in my current role.

In other words, I felt like I was losing my time being here, swimming against the strong current.

When we went to the security office and completed all the needed statements and forms, it was already 6 am. Somehow, I managed to walk to my cabin, trying to rest my feet for a few hours before starting another 15-hour shift. The boat was rocking too much. While lying in my bed, I looked at that tiny, limited space. The baggage was bouncing back and forth due to bad weather. We did not have much extra room in the small cabin, so we tied up our bags with a rope and positioned them next to the small sink in the middle. I never felt so tired. Not physically, but emotionally.

The following morning, I started my work at 10 am, and with two short lunch and dinner breaks, I finished the next day again at 4 am.

With no ability to calm down, I drank some cheap white wine in an attempt to relax.

Finally, I had a chance to sleep for five straight hours after a long time.

Go up or give up

The first month on board, a real struggle. Life onboard makes you feel empty, frustrated with a company system designed to squeeze the life out of you most of the time. But somehow, whenever I felt angry or devastated, I knew exactly how to put those feelings away to provide excellent customer service to the guests. Numerous times, I reminded myself that happiness in life is in our eyes; in our hearts, despite the circumstances, it is the ability to find something good in everything. Happiness is our unique journey, not the destination where we will arrive one day. And despite everything, I still felt content, thankful for every moment, and I consider it a priceless experience.

The key was to act myself into a good mood, regardless of difficult circumstances. Otherwise, giving it to depression would be a dangerous scenario. In more than ten years onboard, I made many people smile. Whenever I felt lonely and without purpose, I would still push myself to smile and instantly make our guests laugh, no matter how hard life on the ship was for me. By doing that, deep inside my heart, I felt as a positive influencer, an inspirational speaker.

Undoubtedly, I have found my lasting legacy. Working on the cruise ship made me a creative person who always sought new ways to overcome obstacles. Whenever I would inspire someone not to give up and keep trying, that gave me this incredible feeling of accomplishment and a strong sense of purpose in this world.

Tips for future sailors

This book has been fully dedicated to all heroes of the seven seas, true warriors who sacrifice their gift of presence to provide a better future for their families back home. The main inspiration behind these pages is my sincere hope that there will be justice in the maritime law regarding working rights in the shipping industry one day. We need laws that do not discriminate because of the position or nationality, but equally implemented laws have the same rules for everyone.

Those fundamental values and correct, sound principles should be priorities for a multibillion-dollar cruise line company. Because in this hectic, modern world, there should be at least one thing more valuable than money itself: ethics.

Ultimately, our success should be measured by how many people we have supported and guided through our steep pathways and how many people we have inspired and influenced to fight inevitable adversity. It is not about how much money we make. Money will often blind us with a clouded, foggy perspective of our reality, and if money becomes our primary priority, it is a matter of time when we will learn the life lesson the hard way.

The cruise ship company owners, all the people, sitting on the comfortable sofa in their air-conditioned offices, are only concerned about the profits, increasing revenues, and reaching enormous targets. They become more and more greedy, money never enough, they want bigger and bigger ships, often at the expense of underpaid crew members. That's all about it. Who cares about the rights of the crew members on the seven seas? Most of the time, crew members do not complain regardless of how complex the circumstances are; they still manage to do their daily tasks. Crew members won't say a single word against management because they will be quickly replaced by some of the many people waiting for their jobs if they do so. There is a high turnover rate, but management seemed not bothered by that. Crew members are being replaced like an over worn sock.

During my career at the cruise ships, I have witnessed that some of the best employees left the company only because of one reason: they did not feel acknowledged for the complex and creative work and for the sacrifice they make every day.

On the other hand, American guests are the best customers globally by far. They are easy to please, and they often show their gratitude towards the crew members' extra mile effort. American people often show appreciation for the service from the hardworking crew members on board the ships. They enjoy talking, laughing, and humour is effortless, simple, and very contagious in a good way. Often, our guests would patiently and respectfully wait for their turn to be served in the bar operation.

The company came up with an impactful idea to recognise loyalty, so they divided all our guests based on their sail and sign card colour. That card was used for all payments and transactions onboard and room keys simultaneously. Guests who were first-time cruisers have a blue card, and all returning guests have either red, golden, platinum, or diamond cards based on the number of cruises they have previously been on. However, few guests who sailed numerous times were the kind of people who usually acted like the ship owners, born with a golden spoon. They were continually looking for innovative ways to complain, even for the ridiculous things that do not make much sense, just to prove they could get whatever they wanted. From the crew's perspective, we were amazed by the level of arrogance of those people, most of the times. The company created these colours for their sail and sign cards to indicate those rude customers' imaginary importance status. As crew members, we should always be on the top of our toes; whenever standard service dropped down for some reason, those people created drama after drama at the guest services desk. They would often treat the crew members like their personal slaves, yet management supported that system all the time.

There was a true, memorable story when I worked at the Lobby bar on Deck 3…

Golden people with rusty soul

It was just a regular day at work for me. My shift had started at 10 am; it was a sea day. The ship was rocking a lot due to heavy winds and strong waves. When I entered my working area, I immediately noticed that the bar counter was hammered; 50 people were waiting to be served, and only four bartenders were on duty at that time, including myself. Quickly, I took a couple of orders and greeted everyone with a smile on my face. Suddenly, while I was shaking cosmopolitan martini, one of the guests put his card in front of my face and said to me, "Don't you see the colour of my card! I was supposed to receive a VIP service here. I have more than 50 cruises with this company for your information, and I am certainly not supposed to wait any longer. This is ridiculous."

Well, without being affected by the arrogance, I immediately replied, "Sir, what is ridiculous is that you are trying to poke my eye to get my attention. Kindly understand that I am not differentiating between your diamond card and the blue card from our valued first-time cruisers. You will be served when your turn comes. It's straightforward. First come, first served. No colours, no preference based on the card colour. Fair treatment for everybody." I concluded my clear and firm statement.

As you can imagine, he was furious. Unfortunately, despite his 'royalty status' on board, he could not contest my equal approach to everyone.

Throughout the ten years career, there were many situations like this. The outcome was always the same. I have seen the crew members being terminated because of those kinds of guests. Those guests often went that far to satisfy the need to feel important. Therefore, they would make up the stories against the crew members. And guess who got company support? Yep, correct. The diamond and platinum guests, not the crew members. Despite all of that, I would still perform at my highest professional standard in 90 percent of the situation. It is part of my job, and I am being paid to do that. Usually, I just put a fake smile on my face and listen to their stories about how much money they have, who they know from company top CEO officials, and how everyone must be polite to them. Along the way, I have learned to put that fake smile on and listen, and that's what most of the crew members did. I understand that from their side, this is a much-needed vacation, a holiday, or a temporary escape from their toxic and hard life, and it is our job to provide them the service that they deserve and create a memorable experience.

Generally speaking, for the crew members on board, we experience extreme feelings every single day. Without a doubt, the worst feeling in the world is when we have to say goodbye to our families and friends every time we leave for work.

On the other hand, the reward for being far away and probably the best feeling in the world is the moment after eight months when we would meet again with our loved ones. However, this is our chosen reality, and we take pride in what we do. Along the way, we meet some fantastic people and create an unforgettable lifetime experience.

I want to share a few tips for the people who plan their cruise, whether you have previous cruising experience or not. Understanding the mutual perspective and treating all crew members on board the ship respectfully is essential. It might help to hear a couple of advice to future sailors.

Rule number 1

Never consider yourself too important when dealing with crew members on board. You are not better than first-time cruisers because you have a diamond sail and sign card onboard the ship, and the company gave you a specific status for your loyalty. We provide equally efficient, friendly service to all our guests onboard the ship, regardless of how many cruises they have been on before. Do not impress crew members with your stories about who you know or where you travel and how everyone looks up to you like a VIP. If you do that, crew members will only provide you with a minimum required level of customer service, and you will never be able to receive some of the best, extra mile hospitality experience. Do not act arrogantly; instead, humble yourself down. You can never be too important.

Rule number 2

Do not bang your card to draw some bartenders' attention when approaching the bar counter on board. Be polite and patient; your turn is coming up in a moment. Important to know because I can guarantee you, if you bang your card while making inappropriate comments about slow bar service, you will wait forever, and the bartender will always find a reason not to serve you. It's an alcohol service policy, and yes, the bartender can refuse to serve you if you show abusive and disrespectful behaviour.

Again, be humble and friendly, and for sure, you will receive some extraordinary, memorable bar experience.

Rule number 3

Do not wave with your $1 bill in front of the bartender's nose. No bartender in the world will serve you properly after that. Even if it is a $100 bill, it does not matter at all. That is a massive disrespect to the bartenders because you insult the employee value. And yes, other guests waiting next to you probably have their $1 bill tips ready, so do not consider yourself as a VIP.

Rule number 4

When talking to any crew member onboard the ship, don't ever say, "Do you know who I am?" Or even worse, "Are you aware that I know some important people in this company, so you all make sure to give me the best service." This is just all wrong. By trying to draw attention that way, you will not get what you want, but also, most of the crew members will spread the word about you and avoid you until the rest of your cruise. Nobody cares about who you are or who you know. Just be humble, and crew members will provide you with the experience of your lifetime.

Rule number 5

If someone has told you before to make a lot of complaints while being on a cruise so that you will get some complimentary champagne or chocolate strawberries delivered to your room, please reconsider your plan to be adjusted. By purposely trying to create drama onboard the cruise ship, you will ultimately spoil your own cruising experience. All crew members will target you for your inappropriate behaviour. Experienced crew members on board will easily read your intention, and they will make sure that you never try something similar again. Mistakes and bad things can happen onboard the cruise ship, do not try to take advantage of it.

Rule number 6

Do not ever sit yourself on your own at the table in the dining room. Wait patiently to be seated. If possible, do not complain too much about the food and potentially delayed service because your food is in the cooks' hands, who are usually good friends with your servers. So… Just be nice. Again, patiently wait and even if you ask your question or concerns, do it in a friendly, respectful way. Those crew members are already doing their very best to provide you with an efficient, unforgettable customer service experience.

Rule number 7

Just because you are a guest does not mean that you don't have to smile when dealing with crew members. If you smile while talking to the crew, in return, that will give you a substantial extra mile service. Smile is free, and it makes a huge difference. Crew members will appreciate your kindness, and for them, that kind of guest behaviour is much more important than a few extra dollars.

Because every unexpected extra act of kindness goes a long way and makes a notable difference for every single crew member on board. It will also make a difference for you as a guest because I can guarantee you will receive absolutely the best service of your lifetime.

Rule number 8

The person cleaning your cabin is not a superman or robot. You have to understand that he is cleaning 50 more cabins besides yours. For that reason, show some compassion and understanding before making unnecessary complaints. Crew members will greatly appreciate that, and you will always receive an extra mile service.

For the second, try to imagine yourself working onboard the cruise ship. You are staying in a small cabin that is slightly bigger than a shoebox. Imagine staying in that room with a randomly chosen roommate from some of the many different nationalities on board. Your cabin is so small that you have to put your baggage in the middle of that small room. When the ship is rocking at night, all your personal belongings are bouncing around the room, and you can't sleep properly. Your roommate is probably working opposite working shifts than you, so he would wake you up while getting ready to work himself when you are trying to rest. Imagine that you work eight to ten months every day, 12–15 hours a day. Your free time is over congested with safety meetings and boat drills. You are constantly pushing off the lid of your physical and mental capabilities. You are away from your families and friends for a very long time; you can't see your kids. Imagine that your manager has never received any management training before taking his position; imagine that the same manager makes your life on board much more complex instead of inspiring you and getting the best out of your skills. You see, it's hard to imagine that. Now on top of all that, you are dealing with some obnoxious and rude guests who would sometimes treat you like their personal slave, like they are your owners. Do you think that is a fair situation for crew members on board? Now, if you ever come to any cruise around the world, remind yourself that by being polite and respectful towards the crew members, you can create a huge positive difference for those hard-working people who left everything behind to provide a better life for their families.

Our job is to create a memorable, unique, and amazing experience for all our guests onboard. But equally important is to create a safe and respectful working environment for those heroes of the seven seas. Unfortunately, many things would forever remain behind the scenes, and most of cruise ship companies are only concerned about profit and revenue margins. One thing is for sure; if you are a guest onboard the cruise ship, crew members will appreciate your polite behaviour more than your money. I can guarantee you that.

Chapter 6
Removing the Lid from Our Potential

Sometimes, people will put limits on us. On the land, on the cruise ships, in any environment in this world. The adversity should serve us only as a boost of extra motivation to achieve our desired goals (Covey, 2004). When I was 11 years old, we had a school marathon. Many weeks before that marathon, I ran at the nearby football stadium every day to prepare myself for this race. Determined to win and compete with my limits, I worked hard while all my friends used that time to play with their toys or watch cartoons on television. In the morning on the race day, my teacher came up to me at our meeting point and asked me in front of all the other kids, "John, do you have proper running shoes for this race?" I only had one pair of old clumsy, dusty shoes, the one I was using for school, birthday parties, and playing outside on the street. Ashamed and embarrassed, somehow holding my tears back, I answered, "No, I have only this pair of shoes."

Without any compassion, my teacher added, "Look, John, there are some other kids who are into track and field sport at this time, and they are expected to win this race. Do not get discouraged because you are not going to win today. It is just a fun race, put it that way."

Because of what she said to me, I thought that I would never win. I watched those kids around me with brand new shoes and new sporting clothes. Before I even realised it, I started to doubt my chances.

Somewhere about 100 metres before the finishing line, I realise that I am still full of unused energy. I started running as fast as I could. Shortly after, I took the lead and won that race! All my teachers quickly came up to me, and instead of greeting me, they were in disbelief; with a confused facial expression, they asked me how I managed to win?

We should never let someone tells us where our real limits are. We should never let anyone wrongly convince us that we are not good enough to achieve our dreams. They don't know what we went through to become who we are today!

It's easy to stay productive when everything goes well around us. True life warriors are the people who will produce their best even when life gets bitter. Difficult life circumstances might keep all of us away from achieving desired goals, but in the long run, that will make us stronger; it will lead us to a more resilient version of ourselves (Maxwell, 2009). We should never give up, regardless of the difficulties. Even if we are meant to fail at specific tasks, we should learn how to fail forward. Keep trying. We are capable of achieving miracles in this world. We should not worry about what other people say. If we are only trying to focus our energy on pleasing everyone else around us, that becomes a one-way street, and we are heading in the wrong direction. Pleasing society's expectations will only make us feel empty. We are all much better than that; our potential is limitless.

Great things will happen when we work hard to shape our unique skills. We need to focus on developing our strengths, not achieving crowd expectations. Overcoming our past mistakes plays a significant role in achieving our desired goals. We should never allow ourselves to remain trapped as a prisoner in the chains of our past. We have to get over it, realise that everything happens for a reason.

Even if it does not look like sometimes, we are supposed to be on our way to glory. One step at a time, patience is the golden skill.

Stop chasing money

I have tried my best to stay determined while working on the cruise ships. My goal was to remain focused, refresh regularly, and move on after failure. We often sacrifice the precious moments of today by recalling past events that we cannot change anymore or worrying about the uncertain future that might not even arrive.

Social awareness is essential, but we should stop comparing ourselves with others in this world. Indeed, we are perfectly created – unique, strong, skilled.

Should we all be pilots, doctors, lawyers, sports superstars, pop singers? Are those missing pieces of real recipes for achieving lasting happiness? Maybe for some people in this world. For those people who have a 'destination' disease.

We should chase our unique passion for leaving a lasting legacy in this world. What drives us to get up from our bed every morning? What picks us up after our failure when we get hurt? If we did not find that motivation yet, it is hidden deep inside our hearts. We need to look harder, go into nature, relax, and spend some time in silence. We should create an environment where we will be inspired and discover our greatest gifts. Because when we do so, at that very moment, life will change forever. Ultimately, we will put ourselves in a position to create an amazingly positive difference in this world.

Money does not make a lasting impact on our happiness, indeed. It is only a temporary relief that leaves us in our comfort zone. Real, permanent happiness is all about finding our purpose. Money comes afterward as a natural chain reaction. While being on the cruise ships for a long time, I wondered what we were all doing better than anyone else?

Indeed, we all have some unlocked treasure, unique gifts that are yet to be discovered. That specially crafted gift will lead all of us to the road to true happiness. Once found, it will show us our real meaning in this world; it will bring lasting joy to our life. When we experience setbacks, we move on, simple as that. Things happened; we accepted the temporary pain, held our breath for a few seconds, got up back on our feet quickly, and try even harder.

We all need to accept the fact that perfection does not exist. What matters the most is that as long we keep trying, keep moving forward regardless of any circumstances, it is only a matter of time to succeed.

While working on the cruise ship, I have adopted one positive mindset – I want to think about 1 million reasons why something will work, not 1 million reasons why it won't work.

No matter what life throws in front of us, no matter how hard life will hit on us with the most challenging shot, we shall preserve for the sake of our lasting legacy. Meanwhile, maybe we cannot control everything that happens to us, but we can control how we react. While sailing through the storm, suddenly, we realise that the shore is closer than we thought. At the end of the day, we will find a way; or we will always find an excuse. It's our call. The future is waiting.

Chapter 7
Lack of Authentic Leadership on Board the Cruise Ships

Days were never-ending; it seemed to me like that, two long months since I signed on. My new working schedule was at the nightclub. It was a very demanding schedule; during the day, I was working in other bars around the ship, and in the evening, I was in charge of the bar operation in the nightclub.

The nightclub was one of the busiest bars onboard the ship. Most of our 5000 guests onboard would visit nightclub bars during their seven-day cruise. Somehow, I liked this work because things were happening very fast. My job was to provide quick, polite, and efficient bar service to the passengers. Being a bar supervisor, I was responsible for overseeing the entire bar operation and ensuring high standard performance. During the busiest hours, we would have at least four bartenders and eight bar waiters in that area. Our job was to work as a team, and when it came to guests' issues, we always supported each other.

A considerable part of my supervisory role was obtaining the strict RSA rules at all times. It was sometimes difficult to call on which guest we should refuse alcohol service.

Usually, that will happen when the fellow guest had a little bit too much to drink or became increasingly aggressive, abusive towards our colleagues or other passengers. It was my job to handle those problematic complaints, and I did that well by politely and firmly convincing passengers that they had a little bit too much and that it was time to have some water instead of alcohol.

It is not what we say; it's how we say. American and Australian guests are by far the best customers in the world. Generally speaking, they are simple, easy to engage, friendly people. They always show their gratitude for our hard work on board the cruise ship. European guests are more distanced, cold; they want privacy, and it's our job to recognise and meet their expectations. American and Australian guests are also much more generous than Europeans when tipping crew members. It's part of the culture, I guess.

While performing a duty, the crew member can make a technical mistake in the bar service, but the foundational rule is one exception. Always smile, do not look serious. Ensure your smile to the guest consistently; no other rule in my job carries such importance. You could potentially drop your bar tray full of drinks on some grumpy guest, you could forget someone's order and leave the guest waiting for one hour, make sure you smile all the time, and everything will be okay.

Now, that sounds a little bit too perfect, but we are all humans. We all have good or bad days, sleepless nights, we don't see our family for seven or eight months, and sometimes it is tough to put that smile on – especially when dealing with rude and obnoxious guests, which happens daily. Sometimes I have smiled sincerely; sometimes, I have to put a fake smile on. It's not easy to wear a fake smile for a long time, but sometimes I have to protect my job. No matter who we deal with on the bar counter, we make sure that smile is on.

Injustice at sea

In the nightclub, bar service is slightly different from other areas on the ship. Due to guests' huge traffic at the nightclub's bar counter, we are time-limited with every order we take. That leads to quick, accurate service rather than endless talk with our respectful guests – which is the case in other, more quiet bars on the ship. Sometimes we had a smooth night; sometimes, it was rough. It takes a lot of effort to remain calm in the early morning hours when making the last call for the drinks in the nightclub.

Preferably, I would always choose to work in the nightclub other than other bars on board the ship. Somehow, I felt that most of my people skills were utilised in the busy, hectic bar environment. Instinctively, I have always tried to act as a leader, and no matter what happens with the guest, I would always support my colleagues and help them out. Other than that, we did not like our work in the nightclub because most of the officers on board were coming to drink there. With no disrespect to anyone, most officers on board were way too arrogant and rude. They just thought way too high about themselves. Consequently, their behaviour in the bar was the same, disrespectful and silly.

The company had a strict rule regarding guest and crew relationships on board. It was strictly prohibited for any crew member to mingle or fraternise with the passenger on board. Also, the procedure clearly explained that no crew member should dance with the guest on the dance floor, and no crew member is allowed to sit on the bar counter; they could only order a beverage from the waiter serving the tables.

Needless to say, we had more problems and incidents with those officers than with any other guests.

On the elegant nights at sea, we were always busy. The bar counter was packed with guests waiting in line patiently to buy their drinks.

One night, I noticed 3rd officer Luka, he was sitting at the bar counter. He was visibly intoxicated, and he was kissing one of the passengers just in front of the security officer's eyes. Calmly, I approached the officer Luka. "Good evening, sir. To remind you that sitting at the bar counter is prohibited for all crew members, including officers. As you can see, it is also hectic, and we need to leave some space for our guests to approach the bar counter. Somehow, I have a feeling that you are intentionally breaking company rules, sir, so please leave the bar counter immediately."

Without responding to my concerns and comments about his behaviour, he just laughed and gave me some serious, threatening look that did not impress me at all.

"Sir, I am sure that your English language is good enough and that you can understand me. Leave the bar counter now, please." I made my point once again.

Since he did not want to move from the spot, I went around the bar, close to the dance floor, and approached the security officer observing everything speechless. "Excuse me, sir, there is an officer who is not following the company rules; he is sitting at the guest bar counter and even kissing one guest in front of everyone. Could you please inform Luka that he needs to leave the bar counter immediately?" Instead of a quick reply, security gave me that confused look, like I was talking to him about nuclear science.

Finally, with visible hesitation, he replied to me, "Listen, bro, do us all a huge favour, just pretend that you did not see anything or anyone, it's better for all of us; believe me, Luka is captain's good friend." It was pretty shocking for me to hear that. The obnoxious officer kept sitting at the bar, and he was kissing the guest in front of all other people.

That response from the Indian security officer made me furious; I was in disbelief.

One of the best bar waiters working in the nightclub was Maksim from Russia. He was a friendly and hard-working individual, always on time, and a very cooperative person with a huge sense of urgency. He had a strong sense of job responsibility. Despite his great personality attributes, there was one problem; sometimes he was too friendly towards our guests onboard the ship.

At the exact moment when officer Luka left the nightclub, a couple of older ladies approached the bar counter and asked if it was possible to take a picture with Maksim. I did not have anything against that request, indeed. It was not a big deal, so Maksim approached those two ladies on the dance floor, took a picture with them. After one of the ladies hugged Maksim, they left the nightclub. With a massive smile on his face and a great sense of humour, Maksim came back to the bar. "Hey John, look at me, dude, I am a true superstar; everyone wants to take a picture with me."

Maksim always kept the good spirits of our team.

Unfortunately, he could not even imagine what was about to happen shortly after that. It was about 3 am and just when we were closing down the bar, a security officer approached the bar. “Maksim, can you please come with me? The chief security wants to talk to you, nothing to worry about.” Maksim looked shocked, surprised and a bit scared. I told him that he had nothing to worry about, to go with them to the security office, and everything would be okay.

It was 4 am when I finally closed the bar. Dragging myself on the way to my cabin, along the crew corridor, I have bumped into the assistant chief security who gave me some significant and unexpected updates. “Your friend, bar waiter, Maksim, is in big trouble; he just got fired. He was reported for mingling with the passenger in the nightclub.”

It was utterly shocking news for me, and I could not understand why the company fired him that night.

Well, it was not about the company; it was the rotten system, irresponsible individual, a security officer who did not want to do his job earlier with an officer Luka who was sitting on the bar and kissing with the guest! That was the person that should be fired, not the hard-working bar waiter whose family’s future was now jeopardised just for taking a picture with the guests!

Worst of all, I saw what happened in front of my eyes! Annoyed and bitterly angry because of apparent injustice, I came into my cabin around 5 am.

My job the next day started at 1 pm, but before that, at 9 am, I was scheduled for a general safety meeting, mandatory for all crew members. After disturbing events at work, I could not sleep at all. How on earth was it possible that Maksim could be fired? What was the real reason behind that cruel decision? I took a cold shower and refreshed myself, and around 7 am, I decided to go to my manager’s office to get some more information. Our bar manager on board at that time was Emil. Cautiously, I knocked on his door and excused myself politely. “Good morning, Mr Emil. I know you have a lot of jobs to do this morning; I would like quickly to ask you what the situation is with our bar waiter Maksim, why he is getting fired.”

Emil gave me that long and empty look. He looked at me sharply and said, “John, I saw your file; without a doubt, you are one of our most valuable assets in this company. I can see that our guests onboard will mark your name in their positive comments about your extraordinary service. You were also chosen for an employee of the month award many times during your career. But frankly speaking, I think you should work for the Human resource department on board, not the bar department. You see, this is just a job; there is no place for hard feelings. Maksim was fired for breaching the strict company policy regarding mingling with the guests. The security officer who witnessed that event from last night stated in his report that Maksim was hugging the female guest on the dance floor last night around 2 am.”

Huh? I could not believe what I was hearing!

“Emil, this is a huge mistake and misunderstanding! I am the witness who saw what exactly happened last night! The fellow guest only asked to take a picture with Maksim, and she was the one who hugged Maksim shortly after the picture was taken! What could he have done differently in that situation? The one supposed to get fired last night was officer Luka; he was kissing the guest while sitting on the bar counter. Security officers could see that it was just in front of their eyes! That is just not fair!” I almost started to scream in the bar office!

"John, listen… Stop chasing justice for your good. This is just a ship's life; rules can never be applied like in the democratic world outside. It's not about what somebody has done; it's about who has done it. By the way, I just received an email from the captain himself. He wrote that he is very disappointed about how you have behaved towards officer Luka. Captain stated that he even seeks disciplinary action against you. Do not put me anymore in this kind of situation that I have a problem with the captain because of your behaviour."

"What behaviour?" I replied to my manager, ironically! "With all respect, sir, I followed the company's guidelines, rules, and regulations. No crew member can sit on the bar counter, especially on busy nights.

Many of our guests were even looking at Luka to move so they could have ordered their drinks. He did not even bother at all! He was kissing the guest in front of all the security officers on the top! Obviously, instead of condemning the officer's action, the easy prey for the security department was Maksim, who had not done anything wrong at all! This is all wrong! I am the witness!

The bar manager looked at me and said, "John, you cannot be a lawyer on board the ship. It would help if you played smart here to keep your job and survive. The captain is strongly linked with the security department, and he always protects his officers, no matter what they did."

"Yes!" I interrupted him furiously.

"You have just said that the captain was always protecting his arrogant officers! Well, why don't you do the same and protect your innocent employee who is about to be sent home in a few hours! Why are you not being that kind of leader that stands up for what is ethically right? Why are you refusing to fight for a good cause? I have been in this company for ten years and never met such a coward like you!" I slammed the door of the bar manager's office and left furious!

I was committed to fighting this injustice alone and went straight to the Human Resource manager's office. HR manager was from England; I was hoping he would listen to what I had to say.

"Good morning, sir. I am sorry to disturb you early this morning; I wanted to share some details about certain events last night. There has been clear injustice regarding our employees' human rights on board the ship. Maksim has been mercilessly fired for no particular reason. Please help me to pursue justice in this case."

"I wish I could help you really, but…once the security officer reports some incident, that automatically goes into the main shoreside office, and we can't change it anymore. Even that I want to help you, our hands are tied up. Sorry, I am afraid that I can't help you," he concluded his statement.

"What about inappropriate behaviour from officer Luka? How does that fit with our 'strict rules and regulations' on board? With all respect, sir, don't you think that policies and procedures should be implemented in an ethically sustainable way, equally and fair for everyone? For sure, there is video footage that can confirm my statements about what happened in the nightclub? Can we assess those materials somehow? An innocent person is being fired, and you will sit down in your comfortable chair with no desire to help Maksim? I sincerely believed that the Human resource department was all about protecting human rights on board the cruise ship! I was wrong!"

While furiously exiting the HR department office, I briefly saw Maksim, who was taken of the ship. He was in tears.

Injustice has been served without regret. Maybe they won one single battle, but not the war, that was for sure. I was committed to continuing to fight for justice on board the ship.

Maksim was sent home in the shadow of all cruise ship irregularities. The system onboard the deeply rotten cruise ship allowed all this to happen.

After this event, my mission was to immerse myself into profound studies to expand my leadership knowledge intensively and positively impact all crew members' working rights on board.

The following day, I decided to enforce a military style into my life on board. I have decided to spend my free time on personal improvement to read at least two books per week to achieve the desired growth. I did not go to the crew bar, never attended the crew parties. Rarely would I get off the ship in the ports because I spent every spare minute reading the books.

The writer who inspired me the most, who invigorated my leadership change, was John Maxwell. My goal was crystal clear, to perform diligent research and create a unique leadership program that will change the ships' poor management systems. I knew that it would also automatically help millions of crew members worldwide. It was a bold and brave goal but worth trying and sacrificing – my lasting legacy and commitment to change and improve life on board for millions of crew members worldwide. My journey was set for making a significant change in the cruise ship industry.

Chapter 8
Letter to the Company's CEO

In the upcoming eight weeks on board the cruise ship, I have read 20 books about leadership and management. My goal was to educate myself accordingly and create a lasting change onboard cruise ships, positively impacting all crew members onboard. For that reason, I have decided to email the company CEO. Of course, I was unsure if he would ever read my email at all or respond to it. Besides that, I did not inform any of the ship managers about my idea to contact the company CEO. Here is what I wrote in that email.

"Good afternoon, sir. I hope you are well upon reading this email. My name is John. I want to propose a program for creating and developing a more effective leader. It will be called 'Sustainable and Effective Leadership'. The participants will be any crew members in a supervisory and management position. I have been working hard to create this unique project, a specially designed leadership program that suits a company's needs."

The goals and purpose of this program are as follows:

- This is a beautiful and explicit opportunity to learn different leadership styles and effectively motivate and communicate with the front-line employees in multi-cultural organisations.

- This program is unique because its content is based on some fundamental values. It explains the importance of understanding emotional intelligence in the cruise ship environment, working standards, and ethics in this industry.
- This program is a critical part of the company's business strategy in attaining a long-term sustainable business while creating value for all stakeholders.

In nearly ten years working with our company, my long journey was always about creating something special, something of real value that did not exist before. It is my greatest desire. Hopefully, I will have the chance to share and make a positive difference for all stakeholders while introducing this Leadership Development Program onboard the ships.

I had the opportunity to present my proposal to one of the senior officers from the shoreside office. Although the response was tremendous and brilliant in terms of my idea and presentation, I was only advised to apply for a Human Resource Coordinator position. I was also told that there would be an incoming Leadership Program. As much as I am passionately eager to be part of the HR team, I am disappointed to know that I won't be part of the team that will execute and integrate my proposal. I have been fully dedicated to creating the contents of this program. Certainly, with the knowledge and experience, I have proven records of positively influencing my working environment.

I have created several modules for the topics to be covered and created the Program Review Concept and Learn-Apply-Reflect Model, a systematic way to monitor results effectively for the participants. It will mainly be focused on applying learnings and finding the most actionable plan to implement onboard the ships. Thus, I would like to express my desire to use and create a possible new position as an Engagement Manager onboard the ship. As the name implies engagement, my role will be to ensure a supportive working environment onboard, equip leaders with proper tools to coach employees daily, and help all our employees on board grow in confidence to take personal accountability for improving behaviour or skill. As the central part of my job description, I will mainly focus on putting the values that will allow the company's business to thrive. To create a new, more effective working environment, I will be a coach, communicator, and role model as a good leader. With this approach to our employees, our leaders on board the cruise line will become the ones who always seek to understand and only seek to be understood after that.

Our leaders will genuinely care for our employees in daily conversation, and, in the long run, that will establish a strong relationship and create a happy win-win working environment. Our supervisors onboard will learn that the true leader must consistently discover every employee's unique skill set and allocate that talent accordingly to benefit the company. That will help me reach the company's most significant goal to create an inspiring leaders who knows the way, goes the way, and shows how. To create leaders who would understand the importance of emotional intelligence, validation, compassion, and empathy in the workplace.

Leaders who would transfer into a much more supportive, creative stewardship delegation style will significantly increase our employees' level of productivity on board. Leaders who will use this program will learn to build up their motivational skills to consistently inspire all our employees to perform at their maximum capacity. Honestly, I believe that leadership is the process of influence, and with your support, this process will create significant value for all stakeholders.

Thank you for taking the time to read, and I hope you will find this valuable. I look forward to your response. I would gladly appreciate any help and advice from you.

Kind regards, John.

Surprisingly, the CEO replied just in a few hours! I did not expect such a quick response from the company's top official! Usually, senior management can value other people's time. The company CEO could have one million reasons not to reply to my message, yet he did. He probably reached this remarkable career success because of those human qualities.

His response to my proposed project was more than good. The CEO told me that my idea sounds exciting and will personally forward my email to the shoreside senior HR manager. Honestly, his reply to my email was already recognition itself! It showed that project materials contained quality and great value.

During those first months on board, I have completely immersed myself into intense studies, and it seemed that my hard work would pay off eventually. The CEO promised me that someone from the HR department would contact me soon. That gave me temporary peace and inner satisfaction. The highest company official approved my idea. CEO of our company knew that positive change was an inevitable growth step. Invigorated by the great news, I have decided to push myself into studies deeply and prepare my presentations to perfection.

Meanwhile, my work as a bartender on the ship continued. It was an opportunity to walk to talk during the busy days at work. When it comes to new learnings and diligent research that I have conducted, I tried to implement those new skills practically and share them within the workforce. In excitement for my upcoming project that suddenly became important for the company, I went to sleep happily in the night, dreaming of the day I could improve management onboard the cruise ships and automatically help millions of crew members worldwide.

Resilience at sea

As crew members, we always find a way to be positive and to smile, despite everything onboard the ship. Managers onboard the ship would often forget the essential part of their job description – motivating and inspiring their subordinates. Instead, they have a different mindset – when a crew member does a good job, it's only part of their salary package. Generally speaking, people on board don't feel validated and acknowledged for their job. Yet, they still do it on a day-to-day basis because they have families back home and need to take care of them. Now, don't get me wrong; a great part of working on a cruise ship story is a challenging, unique, and often life-changing experience. But when you are overly excited about the cruise ship's job, do not expect to chill out on the exotic beach with a beer in your hands, and don't trust the agent who is only trying to get their commission within your employment.

It is challenging to adjust on the first day onboard when we sign on the cruise ship. Depending on the position, you must work 10–15 hours per day, seven days a week, during seven to nine months, but your 'time off' can be very challenging.

When you finally go to your tiny cabin, there are plenty of loudspeaker's announcements for the safety drills, tests, guest services, and even if you are not part of those events onboard, the sounds are annoyingly present in your cabin. In your time off, almost daily, you are scheduled to go through mandatory safety meetings, various drills, and safety exercises for the actual emergency on board, department meetings, and other things.

What crew members have left, it's just a couple of hours of sleep, working consistently under tremendous pressure, and ineffective management on board.

I have witnessed many injustices throughout ten years of my working experience onboard cruise ships. Most of the time, crew members were just the numbers and nothing more than that.

Most crew members are scared to speak up and fight for their rights on board because they know that it might jeopardise their job security.

Unfortunately, I have witnessed many unfair dismissals and terminations of very loyal and hard-working crew members. That decision was brought up by inexperienced, biased managers who would terminate the crew members because of subjective, personal reasons. Meanwhile, in the past ten years, company growth has been astonishing. Truly amazing. It became the wealthiest and the most enormous cruise line corporation globally. The cruising industry has become so demanding that our guests book their cruises, sometimes even a year in advance! But what happens with crew members meanwhile? Extremely hard-working crew members brought up the company's growth, yet no law was ever placed to clarify and support the crew's rights, give them a sense of job security, or make them feel that they are not just the numbers at sea? How do I know that – you might wonder? Because I have seen extreme injustice, unfair treatment. Every day, I could witness the hidden, silent abuse of the crew members.

Also, some of the toughest jobs on earth exist on the cruise ship. Galley steward. The person who would potentially apply for that role probably sounds pretty fancy 'galley steward'. People cannot even picture out in their minds what kind of job it is. If you have ever been on one of those giant cruise ships, you probably know that every ship has two main dining rooms.

There were huge galleys between those spacious, fancy dining room areas, where all utilities were washed, plates, cutlery, and glasses. The galley steward has a tough job – deep cleaning and cleaning thousands of dirty dishes in very humid conditions.

Without a doubt, those crew members are the true heroes of the seven seas. On average, 10–14 hours of consistent, backbreaking work, seven days a week for nine straight months. No days off, no sick leave, no annual leave. That is around 300 hours of work monthly when you do the math, yet galley stewards are paid 450 dollars a month.

Some people might say, but they have an option when they sign up to do that job? But how about those poor crew members' ongoing and excessively abusive management? On a larger scale, who would even question those untrained, shallow managers, the ones who would scream and shout on galley stewards, treating them like animals, while the company officially promotes 'show care and respect' values on board? Very sarcastic, indeed. It is easy to make a policy that should blur the public's perspective, but it's hard to walk the talk. The very unethical money-making process makes dollars and achieves the targets. Who cares about ethics and fairness? That is not of primary importance for the company.

Chapter 9
The whipping of slaves

While passing through that colossal dining room galley, I have witnessed a lack of management and human skills at the worst possible level.

Walking through the entire galley between two dining rooms usually took a couple of minutes. My face was already totally wet because it was way too hot over there.

Now, imagine that you have to spend 10–14 hours in those inhuman conditions? While I was passing through, all of those stewards were kindly saying 'Hi' to me with a huge smile on their faces. When I walked past my friend from Indonesia Gede, at that moment, one Indian galley supervisor was shouting at Gede because some plates were not washed properly.

Politely, I called the Indian galley supervisor on the side and probably surprised him with the following question, "Sir, do you have any personal problems? Maybe some other way to possibly explain why you are yelling at Gede? Do you know that people can often hear only your loud voice when you shout, but not the words you say? You are entirely losing your point with that approach. If I ever again see you being abusive to these hard-working people, I will report you to the HR department." I concluded my statement angrily.

The Indian supervisor did not say a single word. As I approached him a little closer, I intended to scare him. He just walked away. We are very straightforward Balkan people, and we never hold back. Others on the ship are the opposite, the majority of them. They will smile at your face and look for the opportunity to set you up for trouble. I was allergic to that kind of behaviour because I always liked the straight talk and constructive criticism. The company did not like that; they only needed their loyal dogs to implement cruel management policies on board.

The very same afternoon, I went to speak with a Human resource manager about that incident. While explaining my point and clear perspective, I was told by the HR manager that this is classified as 'normal ship communication in such a busy working environment'.

Wow. It took me a while to process that. I have realised the true meaning of HR management on board at the exact moment. That position was designed to protect only company interests and cruel policies and procedures, not individual crew members.

Somewhere between the lines, that situation truly got me thinking. With the burning fire, I still had a vision of changing that cruelty onboard. I have decided to create a unique, specially designed Leadership Development Program focusing on quality training of all managers and supervisors fleet-wide. The goal was simple, to create a happy, win-win working environment where every crew member on board will feel important, acknowledged, and validated. I have studied hard for several months and performed some diligent research in this area. I was excited to find a solution for abysmal management onboard. I fought hard to find a way and to impact the lives of thousands of crew members fleet-wide.

Effectiveness before efficiency

The main topic of my proposed program was 'Sustainable and Effective Leadership'.

These days, most supervisors onboard the ship would delegate the tasks with efficiency goals in their minds, but they don't understand that efficiency we can do with things, EFFECTIVENESS we do with people!(Covey,2004) This is why most of our employees would never be in the most productive version of their capabilities; this is the reason why many great employees with considerable potential would leave our company. It is not because of money but because of the climate made by ineffective communications with their supervisors.

We are all creative-minded people, skilled, and we should know how to lead our teams to their maximum capacities – striving to become compassionate, emphatic leaders who would create an environment where everyone would consistently produce their best, even without being monitored. We can inspire all our subordinates and always find the best conflict resolutions, either for the guest or crew members. Those proactive leaders should be made through this specially projected training that I designed to give my modest contribution to the cruise line industry.

Delegation

Often, employees will feel extra pressure from the ship management style, and in the long run, they will become less productive at their work. The gofer delegation is always focused on methods, and it's not creative. The other, more creative left-brain style of the delegation that I was promoting on board was 'stewardship delegation'. It does have a significant difference in terms of approach and allocating the tasks. Instead of methods, this is a result-driven management style, where we should empower trust with employees. It takes time in the beginning, but it's time well invested. Stewardship delegation involves clear, upfront mutual understanding and commitment regarding expectations (Covey, 2004). It clarifies guidelines, resources, accountability, consequences, and desired results.

The following question got me thinking: Can we impose a gofer style of delegation on the cruise ship and physically monitor our entire crew's performances? Can we be at two places at the same time? Not possible, indeed. Standards and procedures are made to be followed to protect our safety, achieving our daily, monthly, and yearly goals and targets. However, management cannot be all the time supervising every single staff member and run around from one employee to another to tell them, "Do this, do that." Our efficiency will be questioned if we do so. Our employees will reach burnout; they won't feel trusted, validated, and acknowledged for the job they do. By creating and transferring our management style to the stewardship delegation, we should invest our time building trust with every crew member in our teams. Management should become the one who will always seek to understand and only seek to be understood after that

(Maxwell, 2009). We should also encourage an open-door policy and share transparency regarding company goals and expectations. We should look for a way to discover a unique skill set that every employee has, promote people, and make them feel important. If we make those crucial steps, crew members will become proactive even when management is not around. When we build trust and clarify company goals, we will undoubtedly impact the working environment. We should be transparent about financial targets, goals, and expectations. It is also much needed and appreciated to offer our guidelines and sincere support in obtaining the crew's daily tasks.

Enthusiastically, I could imagine being a leader of a team of 20 highly motivated, skilled, and consistently determined employees! This team can achieve any given task and reach any company goal because they feel part of the win-win mindset. Win for themselves and win for the company. When the company acknowledges crew members with deserved praise, we all go a long way toward developing the relationship to determine our project success.

Sometimes, I like to ask staff members, 'What was the best work experience you had last year?' Then I would study their answers and work hard to intensify and replicate those circumstances as widely as possible.

My goal was always to inspire. Putting the extra in 'ordinary' might help the company a lot. The recipe is straightforward. The way to get ordinary people to do extraordinary things is to develop practical habits. We can either inspire and motivate all these people working away from their loved ones or let them perform at the 'minimum required level', just good enough to keep their job safe.

How powerful is that? The slight difference in our daily approach can lead to the highly increased productivity of our employees. I am not talking about financial rewards, not talking about threatening our employees with their job security. I am not talking about being a strict boss to keep our staff on their toes. I am talking about a new level of effectiveness. How do we get the best out of our teams? And even more importantly, how do we maintain high performance standards? How do we inspire people daily?

Those are the questions that will determine the company's future.

Same person, different results, compassion as a key

Let me share the story about one bar waiter I worked with on one of the cruise ships a couple of years ago. This is a true story about the importance of validation in the workplace.

Once upon a time, a bar waiter was working his second contract at sea. He was extremely friendly towards the guests and fellow crew members, proactive in upselling beverage products. Excellence was his usual standard of service. He was always early and presentable at work, polished and enthusiastic. Actual role model, I would say.

He was the best seller in the entire bar department during his first month at work. He would hit all the targets and quickly broke new sales records. He was focused, passionate, and energised. Realistically, he was a great asset to the company; many of our guests came back to the cruise to see this bar waiter again. You can tell by my story that any company in the world wanted to have this dedicated, efficient employee.

One day, his manager came up to him and told him:

"You have missed your safety training again, one more time, and you will be terminated."

After saying that, the manager just left. The following day, it was a sea day. The bar manager called the same bar waiter in the office and, once again, overly reprimanded him, "Next time when you forget to sign your name for linen change, I will give you a warning, straight away."

Undoubtedly, some policies and procedures were to be followed in this case. Especially from the manager's point of view, there is a required code of behaviour, a certain standard to be followed. But out of nowhere, the bar waiter lost his motivation and desire. He felt burnout and unhappy because he was never validated and acknowledged. Also, he felt that manager would talk to him only when there was a problem. Day by day, he felt more intense burnout; he came late at work, stopped shaving, and decreased sales. Even his well-known name from customer feedback comments vanished. Unexpectedly, he became very ineffective at his work. He lost his motivation, self-confidence. The ability to perform under pressure was gone.

The next day, he returned to the bar manager's office without a lasting desire and willingness to climb uphill battle and told his boss straight, "Sir, I don't want to work here anymore. If you don't allow me to change the department on the ship and go to be housekeeping, I will resign."

The bar manager answered, shocked, "Housekeeping? Boy, are you crazy? Boy, calm down, okay? You will be the only person in the company history who wants to change from the bar department to housekeeping; you are making more money at this position and still want to change your job???" The bar waiter was firm and persistent. "Yes, I want to change department because I don't feel acknowledged for the work I do; in fact, the only time that you would come to see me is when there is my mistake."

The bar manager was quiet and only then realised the valid reason why the bar waiter who used to be the role model for the bar department suddenly shrank his brilliant performance and lost his motivation.

Pain is the currency of our success

The crucial part of my proposed leadership program was developing win-win conversational skills, understanding all company employees' emotional intelligence, choosing the right way to address the issue, and resolving the conflict. The key to quality communication is understanding our employees' emotional intelligence, always considering what we say (Covey, 2004). Still, it's more about the way *how* we say.

Success is always on the other side of the pain; we all need to get out of our comfort zone to progress in any field that we choose for our life (Covey, 2004). No pain, no gain. Put it this way; if you sit down all day at the table, you will have pain. If you lay down all day on your bed, you will also have pain, maybe a migraine or something else. You cannot protect yourself from having pain. Pain is all around us; sometimes our best friend, it defines ourselves as a natural way of getting stronger. Without pain, we will never learn, never improve, grow, and never succeed in our lives.

If you can't reach your feet with your hands without bending your knees, how would you make progress? Every day you can reach down as much as you can, and soon you'll find that painful spot, and you hold on there. You hold on there for maybe five to ten seconds. In just a few days, you will be a little bit closer to touching your toes, but it will get more painful day by day. If you repeat this exercise for one week and continuously expose your body to pain, you will get better day by day. And ultimately, you will succeed; you will reach your final goal at the very end.

Whatever painful situation in life we all face, it is the same overcoming process. We should hang on there at the sore spot, hold on for a while, and get stronger day by day. Indeed, we will become more resilient, sharper and gain valuable, defining experience through this pain. With a proper warrior mindset, we can face any adversity with a massive smile on our faces!

100 days at sea

My toughest pain was separation from my family. Here are some letters that I sent back home to my beautiful wife.

"It has been a hundred days since I left – a hundred days since I have not seen you and our little angels. Hundreds of tough and long days are behind us now. And still, there are a hundred more days before I will get to see you again. Thank you for all your sacrifices and unconditional love and support every day, for being my beautiful wife and super mom. Maybe we are now apart, 7000 miles away from each other, but our love will always overcome that distance and these challenging days. The happiest day of my life was when I had met you because you are the most loyal, beautiful person who will stand by my side no matter what happens. As I have said many times before, it's easy to stand by next to someone when everything goes well in life, but only courageous people like you would support and inspire me to overcome even the most difficult times. Thank you for that. Happy birthday my love.

Today is a great day. Yes, it is 8 am, and yes, I am still awake, and I didn't sleep for about 48 hours, but I am truly blessed. I went to the crew mess for a quick breakfast, took some raisin toast, ate some bananas, and squeezed fresh orange to avoid getting sick in this hectic environment. I was looking at my food while eating, and I felt thankful.

Thankful to Lord Jesus, who gave me strength and power to survive this enormous challenge. I felt happy because I made some difference here. I talked to many people and listened to their problems. It makes me feel good because I can finally sense my purpose in this world. It's the moments when it's tough that I would often squeeze and produce that best part.

While working today, my friend Made, a galley steward, came up to be my guest at the crew bar. Whenever I would place my dirty plates in a crew mess galley, I would tell Made to come to my bar and be my special guest. Made came today, he sat down in the corner by himself and talked to me. No matter how busy I would get in the crew bar, I would check on Made every couple of minutes and talk to him mainly about his demanding job. Besides that, I always gave him my best customer service skills, bought him some nice cocktail and snicker bars, vitamin water, and chips. And today, while I was joking with him, he told me, "John, I don't have anyone here on the ship; thank you for being my best friend. You inspire me always."

It's hard to put in words how much it meant to me to hear that statement. It was a fantastic achievement for me, more important than any material thing. My legacy is to serve others.

A few days ago, bar steward Nyoman, a very hard-working person, told me the same thing. I went to speak with the HR manager about his situation. Somehow, he is already in the seventh contract with the company and still a bar steward; no one cares about promoting him to the bar waiter position. We practiced his speech before Nyoman approached the bar manager and asked to be sent to the bar college, but after we practiced a few times together, he was still rejected by the bar manager when he went to the bar office.

Instead of showing support for Nyoman's future in the company, the bar manager told him that, unfortunately, all positions are locked at the moment due to having extra people in our department. When Nyoman returned, and told me that I was not happy with the outcome, I spoke with the HR department. I have explained to the HR manager that it is unfair for Nyoman to be stuck in the same position for years and not get a chance to progress because the company can't find an appropriate replacement for such a difficult bar steward role. And finally, after intense work, one of the HR people told me that Nyoman had been scheduled for the talent plus test and that soon he would be promoted to the bar waiter position. I would often pay him extra for the hard work that he does to help in the crew bar, and he is always so thankful for that, but when I told him the big news that he is going to be promoted soon and that he is already on the list for talent plus test, he started to cry in front of me. But those were the tears of joy. He told me that he would never forget what I did for him and his family.

Things like this are the most valuable assets of my life. My true legacy in this world is finding a way to inspire other people to become the best of their abilities. I can't wait to see you, my love!

Chapter 10
A Broken Piece of Glass

Four months onboard seemed like an eternity, but I have managed to survive. Indeed, that was an accomplishment itself.

Daily work became increasingly stressful while waiting to hear back from the company headquarters regarding my proposed project. After four months on board, I was scheduled to work in the lobby bar. What seemed to become a daily work routine was about to change one night at sea.

It was a rocky, stormy, but elegant night at sea. All of our guests were dressed up for the occasion, looking forward to creating some unforgettable memories on their voyage. The lobby bar was different from any other bars on the ship because of the demanding and picky guests. Most of those guests in the Lobby bar had platinum or a diamond sail and sign card. For sure, it was not my favourite working area at all. Those spoilt diamond guests wanted continuous entertainment on the bar counter, and I often had to force myself to be their clown. Many fake smiles every day to keep my job safe; it often made me feel pain in my cheeks.

Indeed, there were also some lovely guests in the lobby bar, but most were not humble. The arrogant attitude was the predominant behaviour code at the lobby bar.

It was almost 7 pm. Two other bartenders went on their dinner break, and I have stayed alone. Shortly after, a group of twenty guests approached the bar counter at the same time. Despite my experience, it was a challenge to decide who gets a bar service first.

"Good evening, folks. Who was next in the line, please?" Politely, I asked them this essential question. Somehow, I have managed to maintain expected high service standards, despite a bustling evening.

Elegant night on board was when the lobby bar usually gets packed with the guests. It's a special kind of bar where guests sit down for several hours and talk to the bartenders. The type of guests would observe every move I made inside the bar. They were looking at how I am preparing those drinks and where we keep the fruits, sodas, juices, and wines served at those busy times. It was annoying and disturbing for me, working hard while being scrutinised by those guests looking for little things to complain about. After ten years onboard the cruise ship, I have learned about the guests' significant demands and service priorities. To earn my monthly salary, I had to deliver fun and create a memorable customer experience at all times.

On that busy night, for some unknown reason, I had stayed entirely alone in the bar. Other bartenders went on their scheduled break, but still, they made a mistake because, in the bar department, we should never go at the break if it is a busy time and let our colleagues suffer on their own. Especially around 7 pm, many random guests were strolling around because the lobby bar was located next to the busy dining room area. At one point, I got hammered. 20 of my valued guests approached the bar counter simultaneously, trying to order their drinks.

I was an experienced, quick, with the snappy movement around the bar, yet it was not enough; I have got slammed. My colleagues left me on my own to deal with an unpleasant situation, managers and supervisors were far away to help, and I did not even have the time to pick up the phone and call for support. Of course, in this kind of situation, the guest will always order the most complicated drinks to be prepared. Those kinds of drinks required a longer period of preparation time. To keep everyone happy, I had to smile contagiously to avoid complaints, so I did. I took as many orders as possible and told my remaining guests that I would be right back in a minute. The most important thing was to make eye contact with everyone and smile to recognise guests' presence at my bar. I was shaking the cocktail with one hand, and with the other hand, I was placing the napkin in front of the guests. Rapidly, I moved around while sweat was dripping off my chin.

"John, are you supposed to get some help here." One of the guests noticed my extraordinary effort to accommodate everyone at the bar.

"Yes, sir, my colleagues will be here shortly, I hope so," I replied with friendliness.

With those circumstances, my job was to prioritise certain activities to achieve the unachievable. I was running around like a chicken, made some fantastic cocktails, smiled, and joked with everyone, always keeping in my mind that I couldn't afford to look stressed in the eyes of those guests.

Frankly speaking, it was not their fault because I was left alone in the bar. Some of them who had already got their drinks were still sitting at the bar counter, enjoying my show and spontaneous entertainment. To avoid any unnecessary arguments, I never decided who was next in the line to be served; that would be such a catastrophic mistake. When finishing one guest's service, I would politely turn towards all other people who were waiting for the drinks, and I would kindly ask them, "Who was next in the line, please?" That way, I would let them decide who was next, and it was a beneficial tactic not to offend any of my respectful customers. Usually, the guest would decide who was next in the line.

The bar counter was getting messy, but I did not have time to clean it because I prioritised tasks. Quick service was a significant priority. When I thought that everything was under control, and when all of the guests on the bar counter were happy and set in good moods, things were about to change drastically and unexpectedly.

An elderly couple approached the bar counter, and they were about to order their beverage. The first impression, they looked rude and intimidating. "Does anyone work here at this bar? Can we order some drinks, maybe today?" The gentleman approached me.

"Good evening, folks, sorry about waiting a bit longer, just give me a moment please, I will be right back." I kept calm and still replied smoothly to their concerns, not giving them any further reason to complain.

They looked just like people who wanted to make drama and complain about anything.

Even more, I have decided not to give them any reason for that. It took me years to master that skill, yet it was not enough.

When I finished serving other guests, I politely returned to the older couple, and surprisingly, the grumpy old lady threw her diamond sail and sign card in front of my face.

"Don't you see that we are VIP guests here? Do you know how many cruises we have been on before? We should be served immediately upon approaching the bar counter, do you understand that?"

To hear such statement, I was burning from inside. Naturally, I wanted to teach them good behaviour, but self-control was much needed, and somehow I remained calm and professional.

"Madam, I am sorry to disappoint you, but your diamond card does not make any difference for me. To be more specific, it does not make a difference if you have been on 100 cruises before and have a diamond card, or it is just your first cruise. We operate in this bar based on a simple rule – first come, first served," I replied with a vast, sarcastic, and fake smile on my face.

"Now, may I kindly take your beverage order? What kind of drink would you like to have? May I suggest some refreshing tropical cocktail?"

It was quite like a comedy show at the bar counter because about 20 other guests were sipping their drinks while listening to our conversation. That gave me an extra boost of self-security; most of the other guests were smiling and giving me the kind of look that said,

"Dude, how could you do that? This woman is just nasty and horrible!"

Well, they did not say that, but I could see it by their facial expression. I have quickly and professionally prepared strawberry mojito for an old, grumpy lady and double jack and coke for her husband. While placing their drinks on the napkin, I gave them a huge fake smile and told them to enjoy it. Other guests at the bar knew me already by my name, and some of them were raising their glass in my direction.

Everything at the moment seemed tremendous and under control; I was at the top of the game. My responsibility was to maintain that positive bar mood with my funny and exciting stories. Suddenly, I heard a scream from the grumpy old lady like the lighting from the clear sky.

"There is a sharp piece of glass in my cocktail! Bartender, you put me in huge danger; what could have happened to me if I drank this? It could become tragic! This is ridiculous. You will pay for what you just did! I will make sure that you will lose your job!" She was screaming louder and louder at me.

Now, let's put the facts first. Straight away, I knew her plan. Being responsible for one of the busiest bars on the ship, I ensured safety in the lobby bar. A neat procedure of washing all the glasses and the ice machine with precision. There was no flipping way that piece of glass could end up in the guest beverage order.

Calmly, I have approached the lady. "Madam, just calm down, please. My significant role here is to ensure your safe and memorable experience in this bar. If that piece of glass was in your cocktail, accept my most profound apology."

My kind words were meaningless. She kept firing at me, "It's too late; I will make you pay! My husband is a famous lawyer; we will sue you." Other guests who were witnessing this occurred conversations were listening in disbelief. At that challenging moment, my goal was only one, to remain calm until my manager arrived. Strangely, it took another 20 minutes for my manager to show up at the scene. While waiting for him, I was exposed to pretty nasty comments from this challenging customer. Well, it's still part of my job, I thought. I can't please everyone, indeed.

Finally, after what seemed like a decade, my manager showed up. Honestly, I have been in this kind of situation before, and I knew that my manager would take the guest's side, even his job was to protect his staff members. When the lady saw my manager approaching the lobby bar, she only got louder in her nasty comments. "Your bartender almost killed me with this." She was showing the piece of sharp glass in her hand. "If you are a good manager, you will know that we are a diamond guest and that it's your job to ensure our expectations are met all the time during the cruise. Also, it's your job to make sure that this bartender will be terminated instantly," she concluded her nastiness in style.

While my manager was preparing to reply to her, one of the guests who was witnessing the entire situation stood up from the bar and loudly said, "It's enough! This is all bullshit! I am tired of listening to this old, grumpy bitch! Do you think you are a big deal with your diamond card? Do you think we are all impressed here? Nobody gives a shit! By the way, John here is the best bartender that we have ever seen; any of the guests onboard will confirm that! But you came with your dirty plan, to create a drama and to show your arrogance in front of all other guests who are just trying to enjoy their time and relax in the silence here in the lobby bar," the guest concluded his angry statement.

My manager was speechless for a moment. Undecided about what to do, he gave me a sharp, threatening look, like this was all my fault. Finally, he called me on the side and said, “John, you need to know how to take care of our diamond guests. This will be a big drama now, and you should prevent it from happening. An investigation will be happening about this case. Security officers were on their way,” he concluded.

Not long after, the chief security and hotel director showed up at the lobby bar.

Meanwhile, my colleagues, three of the new bartenders, came to the lobby bar to replace me. The manager told me to wait for him in his office in ten minutes, while he talked to the lady.

Shortly after, the hotel director, bar manager, and chief security asked me questions about our diamond guests. Interestingly, a bar manager who should support me, did the opposite instead. “The company will pay the price because of your mistake. You should double-check before you served that drink.” He accused me without any evidence.

Luckily, the chief security was a little more supportive. He told me that his officers are reviewing the video footage to see what happened in the Lobby bar earlier.

A few minutes later, shocking facts surprised everyone, including the hotel director! While having an intense conversation with senior managers on board, the phone of the chief security rang. His assistant called to inform him about the news.

As the chief security put his phone down, slowly he started to talk, “John, we apologise for all this inconvenience… My assistant just called me and said that the following diamond guest who complained earlier in the lobby bar did something awful. The video footage that the security team reviewed showed when she went in the corner next to the bar, took a small piece of glass from her pocket, and then intentionally dropped it into a cocktail that you made. After some attention, I guess, she was probably planning to sue the company. Investigation about this incident is concluded now," the chief security told us.

My heart was pumping vigorously. This case was over, but I was not happy at all. The hotel director tried to apologise to me for false accusations, but he was not meant to do that. It was my manager. Speaking before listening and withholding positive feedback about my performance, I got used to having a biased manager onboard the cruise ship. Still, it was hard for me to understand that my manager did not support his crew member earlier in the lobby bar. Instead, he rushed to false conclusions and made an unfair accusation. Not to mention that it was already the third month in a row that I had the most positive guest feedback comments, compared to all other bar waiters and bartenders on board. Yet, that was not good enough; I never received any form of recognition or validation. To be completely honest, I did not even expect to get encouragement. But this incident in the lobby bar showed that the diamond guest just wanted to try to create a drama and potentially sue the company at my own expense.

Luckily, the chief security brought the facts at the right moment and proved that it was not my fault. After hearing that I was not responsible for a piece of the glass in the cocktail, my manager was quiet. He did not say a single word until I left the bar office.

Situations like this onboard the cruise ship can test your courage and determination to preserve the rotten management system. Slowly, I was on my way to take a break, and I decided to go on the open deck for some fresh air. When I got on the open deck, I felt lonely. I missed my family and friends. Looking at the ocean brought me some level of peace, much-needed calmness at that moment. I took a deep breath. The smell of the sea was refreshing for my mind and soul. Yet, a couple of tears dropped down in the ocean that I did not even notice it. I am strong, and I have to do this, I thought, for my family.

Suddenly, while I was in an emotional struggle, I have noticed something glorious. It was windy, and the waves were getting bigger. Standing on the open deck on the fourth floor, I could feel the great waves splashing the boat.

While staring at the endless ocean, something instantly took my attention. Small, tinny flying fish was getting out of the water and flying above sea level. What was spectacular to witness was the course of their flying route. The fish was flying on the lowest possible point above the sea level, and yet, whenever a huge wave would approach, flying fish would amazingly change direction in a matter of seconds. Wave after wave, coming into the path of flying fish, yet, this fantastic little creature managed to avoid getting hit by the huge splash. The flying fish skilfully managed to adjust her course while in the air.

Now, for me, that was inspiring. If that little creature could spectacularly avoid the vast waves, I could do the same.

In the remaining four months of my contract, I promised myself that if a big wave would come across my way, I will instantly adjust my wings to keep flying like this incredible fish.

Chapter 11
Discrimination

Discrimination on board the ship was visible through the bizarre way of dividing all crew members into three categories: officers, staff, and crew.

Yep, I know it doesn't sound apparent. Generally speaking, most of those officers acted like they were the most important people on the planet. Of course, officers have big, spacious single cabins, they do not lack anything at all. They have a superior dining room in a crew area. Nobody else can eat there beside them. There is an exceptionally equipped kitchen, and a personal chef is cooking the best dishes in the world to satisfy their appetite. Officers also have their server in the officer's mess; the assistant waiter provides them with the service during dinner times. Moreover, a particular member of the housekeeping team is cleaning the officer's cabin. Officers have all guest area privileges, meaning that they can easily walk around and mingle with guests, which is what they do onboard most of the time.

Meanwhile, security officers on board the ship were given straightforward instructions… If they see an officer flirting with a guest on board, they should close their eyes, not report anything. In that case, breaking the company policy is not a big deal, unlike with other crew members, where all policies would usually be implemented strictly and on the spot, with no delay. For some unknown reason, ship culture is established in a way that all it matters is your position and tittle. That will determine your status and life quality onboard the ship.

In the second group, there are staff members. Now, most people who have never worked on the ship probably wonder what the difference between staff and crew is? It's a huge difference. Staff members are part of the entertainment team on board, dancers, the spa team, gift shop, and management. Staff members have much bigger cabins compared to the crew members. They also have a housekeeping cleaner changing their dirty linen and cleaning their living places every day. As well as officers, staff members have their staff dining room where delicious food is being prepared daily. Staff members have a guest area privilege, meaning that they can go in the guest area anytime, eat the food in the guest buffet, order a drink in a guest bar with no special permission. They can also watch the comedy show, enjoy the trivia or play some sports on the open decks.

Now, the third group is where I belong, crew members.

Crew members on board were some of the following departments: housekeeping (between 50–80 people), bar department (between 80–110 people), dining room team (between 80–110 people), laundry attendant (between 10–20 people).

Those departments were an engine of the entire cruise industry, the real heart of the company force. Yet, crew members had the worst treatment on the ship because of enormous discrimination.

We had the smallest cabins onboard. If you are claustrophobic and want to work on a cruise ship, please do yourself a favour and look for another job. There is no smaller cabin in the entire world than what we have on the cruise ship. Speaking about survival tactics in the small places, for me, what made a significant difference is that I went to work on the cruise ship straight after finishing my military service. That certainly shaped me up, prepared me for any upcoming challenges. Often, there was not enough space in the cabin just to put two pieces of luggage. One bag usually has to go underneath the bed, and another one often stays floating in the middle of the cabin, tighten up with some shoelaces to avoid movement when the ship is rocking. Also, crew members eat in the crew mess only; they cannot eat in the officer mess, staff mess, or guest area restaurants.

What was remarkable was that I had gotten in trouble eating in the staff mess a few times, located just next to the crew mess.

That happened on the day when I was working on the pool bar on Deck 10. My break was only from 11 am until 11:30 am. From deck 10 to deck 0, where crew mess was located, it took me nearly ten minutes to arrive, especially on the busy sea days when elevators were continuously busy, going up and down non-stop. When I finally reached the crew mess, it was already 11:10 am. The buffet line was huge; it seemed that all housekeeping and dining room departments came to eat simultaneously. If I have decided to wait in line, it will take me another 30 minutes to get my lunch, and I will be late on duty. Instead, I have decided to go around the corner and eat in the staff mess. It was not busy over there, and I intended to grab a few chicken and broccoli pieces so I could run back to work. Suddenly, someone approached me. It was a food manager. "Excuse me; you are not allowed to eat here; you are 'just' a crew member, not a 'staff member'," he told me firmly.

"Aren't we all crew members on board sir, what's the difference, if you don't mind me asking? Well, then I guess I will stay without lunch for the day because, in the crew mess, there is a line from nearly 50 crew members; I have only ten more minutes of my break remaining," I replied, disappointed.

The food manager did not seem to care at all. It was 11:20 am already, and I needed to go back to work. Hungry and tired, I went back to complete my 14 hours working shift for that day.

The crew members face brutal discrimination on board the ships, more than the staff members and officers.

As a bartender, I have often witnessed what happens to the intoxicated workers on the ship. If someone was being drunk in the bar and reported to the security officers, the outcome and consequences for that behaviour depended mainly on the worker's position. To illustrate what I am saying, here is a practical example.

While working in the crew bar, I have witnessed many injustices regarding the company termination policy. Sarcastically, I have seen many crew members being fired for no reason at all. On the other hand, I have also seen wasted, drunk, intoxicated officers or managers who were just advised to go to their cabin without further penalties, alcohol tests, or any consequences. Crew bar was a wild place. There was only one bar for about 1500 crew members on board where everyone could relax after a hard day at work. At the crew bar,

I worked alone; sometimes, I would get help from one more bartender during the busiest hours. While being crew bartender, I showed care and respect to all crew continuously, with no preference, regardless of their position or status. I did not separate the crew members based on their name tags. Quite enjoyable sometimes, a very stressful job most of the time. Yet, I enjoyed talking to crew members and listening to their problems and issues, especially about a hard time onboard the ship. In other words, I was considering myself as a crew counsellor or advisor, someone who was there not only to serve the drinks but to help and support crew members daily.

My working hours were endless. I would start my job at 11 am in one of the guest area bars on the sea days. From 11 am until 4 pm, I have worked in the busy guest area, not for a single moment removing the smile from my tired face. At 4pm, I had a 45 minute break. It was time to run to my cabin, change my wet clothes, shower quickly to refresh, and have some dinner. Around 4:45pm, I had to be in the crew bar; even the bar was officially starting at 5:30 pm, I needed to come to check my storage delivered to the crew bar earlier in the day. Part of my role was to do opening bar inventory, set up the bar for operation, prepare the glasses, put some ice, check if I was missing some liqueurs, wines, or sodas. From 5:30pm until 8pm, most of my clients were officers and some contractors; they were the only ones finishing their jobs early. I have provided outstanding customer service to all the crew members on board. For me, they were my respected guests. I used to learn all of their names, what kind of drinks they like to order, even their backgrounds, what music they prefer, or what sport they like. I was a DJ at the same time being a bartender.

Usually, most of my colleagues in the bar department agreed that the crew bar schedule was considered a 'punishment' probably the worst place to work from all bars on board. When it comes to my opinion, I never agreed with that. The fact was that the crew members were stressed out all day long, and some of them would come to the crew bar in a bad mood, but that was easy to manage for me. Recipe? Very simple. Smile and compassion. I thought about it this way – crew members are already being exposed to horrible management every day. They are dealing with rude guests daily. They are far from their families, so let me be the difference-maker, someone who would positively impact them.

The galley steward, the lowest-ranked position on board, would walk in the crew bar to buy water or cigarettes, and I would approach them with a massive smile on my face. "Hi Mr Gede, how was your day today? What can I get for you today, sir?" They were constantly confused and smiled back at me. They could not believe that someone remembered their name and smiled at them. What a great feeling that gave me as well, in return.

I knew I was born to become a difference-maker; by having the power to help many crew members on board.

Around 9pm , the dining room and housekeeping team would start coming to the Crew Bar. The problem was that they usually came in large groups, sometimes 30–40 of them simultaneously. For me, that meant more running and making sure that everyone gets service fast. By playing some happy music, I set up the mood in the crew bar. I would kindly explain that I can no longer serve alcoholic beverages for their safety for crew members who had too many drinks.

From 10pm until 01:30am was the busiest time in the Crew Bar. On average, I would serve between 800–1400 drinks per night. The challenging part was the closing stage from 01:15 am until 01:30 am because after 01:30 am, nobody could get alcohol anymore, and in those 15 minutes, many crew members still wanted to order a drink.

To round it up, from 4:45 pm until 03:30 am in the morning, most of the days I have worked straight through, with no breaks at all. Crew bar was just way too demanding for me to have a quick break. I have often witnessed a total personality change from the alcohol impact itself during my work. Crew members who would usually be polite and quiet around 1 am would become obnoxious. The real mess in the bar would start around 01:30 am. Strict rules and regulations enabled me not to serve anyone after that time, regardless of their ranking and position.

It's not easy, indeed. The option is to go to the gym every day or the crew bar to have a few drinks. There is no other way to survive for eight months. The gym was a better option to relieve accumulated negative energy and pump up some winning attitude. Unfortunately, the gym would take way too much power. Somehow, the crew bar seemed an easy way out for many crew members, a comfort zone in the uncomfortable environment.

I took pride in my job; being a difference-maker for all of this hard-working crew gave a unique meaning to my job. Somehow, we all became like one family. Thousands of times, I have heard their problems about their managers on board, their plans, worries, and concerns. And I have always offered sincere advice.

A bartender's job is 50 percent being a good listener and psychologist and knowing that I always pushed myself to be extra nice, even on the bad days when I did not feel like smiling at all. Consequently, my approach to the job did not go unnoticed; in those two months working at the crew bar, I was nominated to be an employee of the month two times.

One day in the crew bar was hectic and eventful. Right after I opened the bar, I've got hammered literally. An officer celebrating some occasion, and Chief Engineer Mateo was buying drinks for everyone. My regular guests, Claudio, Felipe, Mario, we're sitting in their usual spot, the bar counter corner. They were mainly polite and friendly to me as a natural reaction to my professional working attitude. I remembered their names, their preferred drinks would be served before they even order, and I would often set them in a good mood with a few quick jokes.

Yet, on the other hand, they were very demanding and picky with drinks choice. What is ironic is that our guests onboard the ship were not as fussy as some crew members. As a large department with massive bar operations every day, it's always expected to run out of certain beverage items during the cruise. So we would always run out of some wine or beer; that was just a regular thing. Our guests on board never made a big fuss about it; if we did not have a specific kind of beer or wine, not a big deal for them, they would order something else.

Well, some officers in the crew bar were not like that. If there was no particular kind of wine on board, they did not want to choose some of the other available wines, yet, they would instead call our manager to look for that wine around the ship. Sometimes, the manager even took the last bottles from the guest area bar shelves to satisfy those officers' wants. They would also complain about the size of drinks, watermarks on the wine glass, sticky bar counter, and pretty much everything. For me, whatever comment they would say, I took it on the bright side and made a joke about it.

Around 6pm, our business already started to pick up. Dancers on board would stop by for a quick drink before their show will start. More officers and contractors kept coming around that time. One cadet officer, who was still new onboard the ship at his first contract, was overly annoying for me. He would walk himself in the bar, pretending that there were no other people before him in line to order a drink; he just considered himself as the most important person in the world. Of course, I had to teach him a lesson he will never forget because of that kind of misbehaviour. His name was Vicenzo. Ranked as a junior cadet on board, he acted as an owner of the ship.

The bar counter was full of crew members who were patiently and in order waiting to order their drinks. Without much respect for his surroundings, Vicenzo just pushed a few crew members around him and loudly said, "Is anyone working here? I want one Limoncello, chilled with two ice cubes, a slice of fresh lemon on the side, and sugar on the glass rim."

Irritated and offended by his behaviour, I quickly approached him and replied respectfully, "Just in a moment, sir, your turn is coming up shortly." I still kept my cool somehow, not showing inside fire and frustration. I turned my focus to other crew members who were trying to order drinks.

Vicenzo kept being overly obnoxious. “I am the officer, don’t you see? I should be prioritised here in this bar.”

By saying that, he instantly pushed me over my patience limits. Instinctively, I left around 20 crew members waiting to be served and went to Vicenzo.

“Sir, I can see that you have a very high opinion about yourself. That is probably very good for boosting yourself-confidence. But let me remind you something, we do not provide service in this crew bar based on the crew members’ rankings. First come, first served – simple as that. If you have any complaints regarding our policy, please contact the customer service desk. Otherwise, just relax and wait for your turn.” Many more crew members walked into the bar meanwhile.

But Vicenzo still kept talking, “Give me my drink now; I am warning you.”

That was the moment when I completely lost my cool. “Listen, show some respect in this bar; if you don’t care to respect me, that’s fine. But you have to respect all other crew members here; they came before you, yet they will be served before you. You lack good manners, and I am not tolerating that code of behaviour in this bar. Adjust yourself or leave; I have a full right to refuse service of alcoholic beverages to any individual who is not complying with strict bar rules and regulations. It’s your choice.”

All other crew members looked at this arrogant officer in disbelief. Finally, embarrassed and ashamed, he walked away from the crew bar. Other crew members who were still patiently waiting for their drinks, instead of getting aggravated for staying longer, they looked calm and patient.

They were not upset about having to wait for a bit of extra time. Rather, they liked how I managed that arrogant officer.

Around 1 am, I have noticed one group of folks who have got out of control. They were all intoxicated; it was the dining room management team. As they wanted to order more drinks, I kindly refused service due to the strict responsible service of alcohol policy onboard the ship. Shortly after being refused alcohol service, the dining room manager from Romania, Florin, picked up the phone and called the bar manager.

Florin told me that my manager approved one more round of drinks a few moments later, but I was still not impressed.

Calmy, I explained my view of this situation to Florin, "Tell my manager to come here to the bar and to serve you himself if he wants. By the maritime law, I am fully responsible for your safety; therefore, if something happens to you because of alcohol consumption, it will be my responsibility and fault."

Florin was confused and in disbelief; I calmly refused orders from my manager, so he called my manager back, saying that he still couldn't get a drink from me. A few minutes later, my manager, completely wasted himself, walked inside the bar, and without any words, he started to prepare a round of drinks for the dining room management team. My manager was visibly drunk; he was waving left and right while trying to make those drinks.

"Stop doing that," I told him calmly.

He did not say a single word; probably, he could not even talk because he was intoxicated himself.

"Sir, stop doing that; I am warning you; this is the last time. You might be my manager, but you are wrong. You are going against my ethically correct decision to refuse service to intoxicated crew members, strictly prohibited behaviour onboard the ship. On top of that, you are trying to serve Florin yourself. Leave those bottles and walk away from this bar before I report you to security officers. They will bring you to an alcohol test, and tomorrow you will be fired. I don't want that."

I followed him around the bar while he was looking for the missing ingredients to serve Florin and his group. Other crew members witnessed a bar manager act of madness on the bar counter. Despite being drunk, he came closer to me and said, "I am your manager. You do what I say. If you don't do it, you get fired. It's straightforward, boy."

Florin observed the situation, and he gave me that sarcastic, critical look to show that he is happy now. Just when the bar manager was about to put the drinks on the bar counter, I took all of those prepared drinks and threw them in the bar sink, one by one. The bar manager and Florin looked at each other shocked.

At that moment, security officers finally showed up. "What is going on here? We were called for assistance in the crew bar." The chief security approached.

"Nothing major, sir; everything is under perfect control. I was just about to close my bar for tonight anyway," I replied.

Florin and the bar manager did not say anything.

They knew that if we all went to the security office to do an alcohol test, both of them would lose their jobs instantly. Despite being upset at my manager and Florin because of their ridiculous, silly behaviour, I still did not want them to lose their jobs. I knew they also have families back home to feed and still need their jobs. As the bar manager slowly sneaked out of the bar, the chief security approached me. "John, we have several witnesses who confirm that your drunk manager abused you. He was off duty, yet he entered the bar in his civil clothes while entirely drunk. We know what happened here. You did a good job when you refused the alcohol service to the intoxicated dining room manager Florin. Your manager did not have a right to come inside the bar while off duty and attempt to change your correct decision. All we need from you is to make a statement about what happened tonight. Just explain in the details what happened and we will send this statement to the Miami office, and Florin and the bar manager will be taken to the alcohol test tonight."

It was a hard decision for me; one part of me wanted them to be taken to alcohol tests and get what they deserved, which means they would both get fired. Allowed alcohol content while being on board the ship was only 0,08. That is a maximum of two beers or two glasses of wine. They had much more than that, and I knew that my statement would get them terminated. It was a difficult decision, but my human side prevailed in the end.

Security officers were waiting for me to say something and decide the course of action. With apparent hesitation, finally, I told them, "I am sorry, but I don't want to be the person who will be responsible for anybody's termination. I am sure that they deserve that for their unprofessional behaviour in the crew bar, but I don't want their families to pay the high price for their mistakes; they need this job, the same as all of us. I cannot make an official statement against them; I am sorry."

"John, it's okay; they deserve that. You need to know that if you change your mind and come to the security office tomorrow to make the statement, that will not be possible anymore."

"Yes, sir, I understand that. I will not change my mind; this is my final decision; I will not make a security statement about this event."

Shortly after, security officers left; it was 01:30 am, and the bar was closed for the night. It was a tough decision, but I have decided to listen to my human instincts.

The next day, while having my lunch, suddenly somebody joined me at the crew mess table. It was my manager, Emil.

"John… I don't know what to say; thank you for not making a statement against me last night. I had too many drinks; they would terminate me if you made that security statement. If you have done that, it will be the correct decision. Since you didn't do it, I would like to thank you. Accept my sincere apology," he said with an ashamed look on his face.

"Emil, do you have kids?" I asked him in surprise.

"Yes, I do," he replied.

"Well, put it this way, I just did not want your entire family to pay for your mistake from the last night. That would not make me proud and happy; despite everything that happened, I know that you have a family to feed."

My manager seemed to be stunned by my honest words. It was hard for him to learn his new life and management lesson called COMPASSION.

Chapter 12
Emotional Intelligence on Board the Cruise Ship

After four months onboard the cruise ship, I felt tired. I was fed up with dealing with obnoxious people. That's what I have called-the half time diesis.

Luckily, I kept myself focused and determined. My goal was to continue the learning process by immersing myself in profound leadership studies.

While working on the cruise ship, I often had trouble dealing with my own emotions. Sometimes I was reactive to all non-important things and issues.

The key is to have self-control for our improvement, and the most important fragment of that was our emotional Intelligence.

Emotional intelligence is such a powerful weapon. It is divided into four simple categories: 1) Understanding our feelings 2) Managing those feelings 3) Understanding other people 4) Synergy with the rest of the world.

Throughout the years, we slowly learn about our own emotions. The first learning step is to be aware of those emotions (Bradberry, Travis, Greaves, 2009). The second step is to know how to control those emotions. It can take years or even decades to improve in that aspect of our life. After we master those two essential parts of emotional intelligence, we can move on and show compassion and empathy to others – that's what makes all difference in this world, in our personal life, or in the working environment (Bradberry, T., & Greaves, J. 2009). To understand our surroundings and other people, we must first study our behaviour. It is an uphill battle to understand others and not to understand our reactions and emotions in the first place. Understanding others has a lot to do with active listening skills. When someone talks, we should actively engage and show that we care. That is how we gain permanent respect from all people around us. After mastering those three life-changing skills, synergy with the rest of the world comes naturally, like a cherry on the top of a beautiful cake. When we learn how to identify and recognise our own emotions, learn how to deal with those emotions, and show understanding and compassion to others, we are ready to join our energy and knowledge with the rest of the world, to create a synergy for the higher good of this world (Bradberry, T., & Greaves, J. 2009).

Finally, after many years of being a bartender on the cruise ship, somehow, I have learned how to master my self-control in overly stressful situations. Step number one in developing emotional intelligence balance is clearly understanding our own emotions. After we know how we react in those difficult and stressful circumstances, we can only improve the quality of our emotional reactions. After years of dedication to change and improvement, I realised that we could not control the events and behaviours of the people around us, yet we can, and we have to control how we react to it. It's the alphabet of emotional intelligence, not only onboard the cruise ship but also in life. Staying calm under difficult and stressful situations is the pinnacle of our emotional existence. To show compassion and empathy to another person, we need to master our emotions. It's often a decisive factor for survival.

For example, management forces crew members to learn and repeat the day's service values. Something like "Show care and respect at all times". It is even written on the main ship corridors, all over the space. How sarcastic? Managers on board the ship are doing just the opposite. Care and respect are not part of their vocabulary. They are unable to walk the talk.

Generally speaking, there was a specific pattern of management thinking on board the ship – if a manager terminates many crew members, he will quickly get a promotion. It was a widely adopted management approach. There was just a plastic management hierarchy, no open-door policy, no validation for crew members' hard work.

Fighting for sustainable change

Despite all adversity and hardships, I have decided to keep fighting. It was not only for my family but for the rights of many other crew members on board. Indeed, I was committed to making a lasting change for the company. I have dedicated myself to that direction and I gave all of my free time onboard. My dream was to make a difference, and I was ready to pay the price for it.

On the way towards achievement, every goal in life must come through an inevitable road of adversity. It was the same as my idea; the price was pretty high at that time. Besides the fact that I was barely getting off the ship and never went to crew bar or crew parties, I have spent all of my free time on board this ship studying hard, researching, and getting ready for a potential big shot. Sometimes I would read the entire book in 24 hours, which was my commitment level. Day by day, I was getting better at a pure understanding and implementing my idea. Regardless of the people who would sometimes show up as obstacles along the way, my desire for creating the change was sky-high.

Stolen Idea

Days passed by, and no news of my leadership proposal yet. Nobody gave me any information about whether the company will schedule the first 'Leadership Development Program' or not.

One day, my manager told me that another conference call with the office had been scheduled. The senior HR Manager wanted to hear more about this proposed project. Frankly speaking, I was very naive at that time. Indeed, I should not have presented any of my materials and ideas to the company. Especially not before getting some guarantees about the program implementation. The problem was that after ten years onboard, I have automatically developed a strong sense of belonging; I wanted to believe that, meanwhile, I have become an essential part of the cruise ship family. The motivation behind my ongoing research and intensive studies that I have conducted was a belief that the company would recognise my effort and let me be the one who will implement this exciting management project.

On my second conference call with the company senior HR Manager, I stated that money or salary increase was not my motivation to create this Leadership Program. All I wanted was the chance to implement and execute this project and to reap the seeds of positive change fleet wide. The senior HR manager sounded delighted about my idea. He assured me that company never before had such a program for the management on the cruise ship. More importantly, he admitted an undoubted need for immediate, drastic management changes onboard the cruise ships. The company was very much aware of that. During that conference call in the bar office, I was so excited. It was almost too good to be true; all my effort was about to pay off just like that.

Naively, I gave away all materials and ideas in that conference call. There were no guarantees. The company could steal my idea and materials and implement them independently, without my involvement. When the conference call was finished, the HR manager only thanked me for my considerable contribution.

He did not mention that the company was already preparing to implement that Leadership Development Program only two weeks after our conference call. Without a doubt, that was such a complex, heavy hit straight in my face. I felt betrayed by the company. Again, it was confirmation that I was just a number, a casualty of the cruel slavery system.

Indeed, only two weeks later, all ship departments were invited to participate in the mandatory 'Leadership Development Program'. The company, in the end, stole my idea. Yet, I was still somehow happy; personal fulfilment was still there, knowing that my measurable involvement in such a significant management change was like a recognition itself. It was not the most sustainable effort for change from the company's business perspective, but still, I wanted them to succeed. It was necessary because of the crew members onboard the ship, heroes of the seven seas who deserved better management. The change I was proposing was dedicated to them.

Other than that, stealing someone's idea can never lead to lasting success in business. Mark the words from one of the world's most significant innovators of all time, Mr Nikola Tesla, who said, "I don't care that they stole my idea… I care that they don't have any of their own."

Working without pay

135 days on the ship, I missed my family more and more; day by day, it's getting harder. We talked through Skype, maybe three times a week. Those were always the most beautiful moments during my lonely days at sea. It was like a rainbow after the storm.

One rocky and windy night at sea, I finished my job and came to my small cabin. Instead of taking a rest, I started recalling some memories from previous contracts on ships worldwide. One particular contract came to my mind.

My memories brought me years behind in the past. It was 2010. At that time, I was on a cruise ship in San Juan, Puerto Rico. It was my third contract with the Company. Most of our guests onboard were from Puerto Rico, and only some were from Great Britain. As a part of the bar department operation plan onboard the cruise ship, we did not have a fixed salary, only commission from the sold drinks. What was remarkable from that contract was that after seven months of working on the ship, I arrived in my home country with $50 in my pocket. Yes, correct, at that time, back in 2010, I have spent 210 days at the sea while working seven days a week, yet my total savings were only $50.

You wonder how?

Well, let us say, for example, that you are a guest onboard the ship, and you have decided to purchase one beer. It will cost you $7.50, and on top of that, it will be added another $1.13, a 15 percent service fee-gratuity charge. In 2010, most British guests on board, despite being pretty wealthy, did not like to pay gratuity for their servers onboard the ship.

In other words, during the one working day, my sales were usually around $500. With a simple calculation, my earned gratuity for that day should be $75 . Here is why I am saying 'it should be'. While onboard the cruise ship in San Juan, our Puerto Rican and British guests enjoyed the best possible customer service. Polite bar waiters and professional bartenders provided efficient, personalised, outstanding customer service at all times. So why did we work for free at that time? Let's put it this way. Our British and Puerto Rican guests enjoyed the best times of their lives while being our respectful guests onboard and at the same time, but they wanted to pull out their paid gratuities on the very last evening of their cruise. That way, around 120 bar waiters and bartenders on board ended up working for free seven days a week! Pretty shocking facts, you would agree? No wonder the company ships were registered in Panama-company did not have to obey US labour rules and regulations. The sarcastic part of that contract in 2010 at that time; bar staff on board the ship were forced to buy their flight ticket to reach their home country upon the end of their contract. At that time, a one-way flight ticket from San Juan to Belgrade costed $1800. So if you consider the fact that with the guests who were pulling out gratuity, I was making, on average, $300 monthly. It's easy to convert that it took me six months of hard work on the ship to save money only to pay my flight ticket to go home. The company did not care. Dollars kept coming; that's all it matters to them. All bar staff signed the petition against cruel labour rules on board the ship at that time.

We demanded that the company should be paying for our flight ticket at the end of our contract. Paper was signed by all 120 workers in the bar department and forwarded into the Miami office. A few days later, a response message came back from the highest company official: "Company reviewed your request for assisting with the flight tickets to your home country. However, this is not possible due to company budget limitations."

The hotel director, who was also from England, did not seem concerned. At the bar department meeting that was held shortly after our signed petition, he said, "Guys, if you don't like our rules here, you are free to resign any time; just let me know."

How discouraging was hearing such a statement from someone supposed to be a motivating leader for all of us on board the ship during those difficult times? Truly unbelievable. Guests onboard that ship were given the option to remove gratuity without even explaining the reason why. Those guests would probably feel ashamed of themselves if they only knew what damage they had cost for the crew members' families. We worked seven days a week for 210 days straight just for food and a place to sleep. Yet, we still smiled every day onboard, and despite all, we still managed to provide world-class customer service to our guests at all times. On that contract back in 2010, it took me exactly 180 days at work to only buy my ticket home.

Welcome to the seaman's world. The company was distancing itself from crew members' underpayment issues on board. They were even blaming a third party, the agency selling those cruises at that time. The British and Puerto Rican guests simply took advantage of that gap in the company system. Those guests were still paying for their drinks; only our gratuities were pulled out and sacrificed. With no fixed salary, that gratuity was the only thing we counted on. Our hard-earned money was taken away just like that. Indeed, guests were always happily drunk, and the company was happily sober while counting their enormous revenues.

How about hard-working crew members, the most significant company assets indeed? Were we working like a donkey and getting paid peanuts? When I look back at those times, it's crystal clear why and how such a huge cruise ship corporation grew enormously throughout the years. The simple formula of their success was everything but not sustainable. Use the blood and sweat from the crew members to build the giant new ships every year. While working seven months onboard the cruise ship in San Juan, my family also needed support. But who cares? More importantly, why would someone care at all? Working on a cruise ship is everything but not fair. That contract remained like a pure reflection of human greed at its worst, a company that achieved all financial targets at the expense of its crew, the company that failed in the human aspect.

Somehow, with all that bitter experience, I am still grateful. I have learned a lot about myself; it takes to fail forward, band, and stretch to survive. Money comes, and money goes, but lessons from difficult times make us resilient and permanently stronger.

Chapter 13
Pursuing Justice

150 days onboard

It was 5 am when my roommate's alarm woke me up. Gede was a perfect roommate. Despite our significant cultural differences, we were getting along really well. Gede was silently getting ready for work, a morning routine, trying not to wake me up. The heavy, metal cabin door was noisy itself, but when Gede was leaving our cabin, he would slowly close the door to avoid waking me up. He was considerate and respectful by doing so.

My shift started at noon, and Gede started his work at 6 am. By far, his job was much more difficult. Gede collected garbage from 20 busy bars on the ship; it was a never-ending job for him. No interaction with guests, only garbage collection all day long. Yet, Gede was a resilient, strong individual dedicated to his goals, providing a better future for his family.

Honestly, I did not like how the bar management treated Gede. Orders were given to him mercilessly, with no compassion or understanding at all. He was overloaded with an excessive number of cleaning assignments. What's was remarkable is the 'must-do' style of management that promotes cruelty and discrimination.

It was a sunny morning – gorgeous, spectacular views from the bar on the deck ten aft. Aft has a meaning back of the ship in a cruise ship vocabulary. Together with two more bartenders, I was scheduled to work in the Aft bar from 12 pm until 5 pm before taking the break and going downstairs to work in the lobby bar. On sunny days, the Aft bar was literally packed with guests. The reason behind it was simple, it was an adult-only area, and there was four luxurious jacuzzi in that area, so the guest could enjoy their privacy.

Work was consistent, and it was a boiling humid afternoon. Short and friendly interaction with the guests was part of my daily work routine. Ice and soda refiling, beer keg replacements, cost and inventory control, attaining the highest standards of United States Public Health were some of our job descriptions in the bar. Besides that, bartenders supervised four to ten bar waiters.

The assistant bar manager from India observed the entire operation from the corner. Suddenly, he approached one of the bar waiters going around with the tray and started loudly and publicly humiliating his work performance. "You bar tray is a mess! How many drinks did you sell in the past one hour? If you want to keep your job, ensure that your sales are high enough! Get back to work now!" the assistant bar manager screamed at the poor bar waiter.

Many of our guests sipping their cocktails on the bar counter overheard our colleague's horrible treatment.

"Relax, buddy, the waiter you just shouted at is doing a fantastic job all day long." I pointed the finger at the assistant bar manager Rashid.

In return, the assistant bar manager just gave me a sour kind of smile and left the bar scene.

Indeed, I knew it straight away, he left to complain to the beverage operations manager, but I did not care at all. I was fed up with this terrible management style and was ready to face any consequences. When he left, most of my guests on the bar counter were still looking at me, confused. My colleagues were also in disbelief, mainly because I was not scared of the Indian manager. Why would I be? I was just the boy who instinctively ridiculed the slavery regime on board the cruise ship. And I was ready for just about anything to stand by my legacy.

Rashid left the bar ashamed because his slavery regime did not work well in the Aft bar. I did not regret my words at all. In a way, Rashid was my supervisor, but more importantly, I did not like how he handled the bar servers in the Aft bar.

Technically speaking, Rashid lowered the company rating because he shouted at the bar server in the guest area in front of many passengers, which was disgusting. One of my favourite guests, Mr Jo, shook his head in disbelief and said to me, "What a prick, that guy in a white uniform. How does he dare to treat poor bar servers like that, especially in front of many of us who witnessed his arrogance? If any of us can help with a statement or support your side of the story on the customer's service desk, we would love to help. We hope you will not end up in trouble; that guy looks like he was after making some drama."

"Thanks Jo, you are awesome, dude. Honestly, I could not help it; sorry that you have to witness that."

"Rashid represents the slavery systems onboard; apparently, he is missing a whip in his hands. Frankly speaking, I am not setting out for that arrogant attitude. It's below acceptable behaviour, I am also a bar supervisor; my job is to ensure quality customer service for my respected guests, and I am not going to let this manager disrespect my colleagues here." Enthusiastically, I have concluded the statement and justified my earlier action in front of all the guests.

Shortly after, the Aft bar phone rang. It was my manager Emil, who wanted to see me in his office in no time. Remembering that moment like yesterday, so many guests wanted to go downstairs to support my version of the story. I politely thanked all of my lovely guests, who were just a bunch of great folks!

A couple of minutes after, calmly, I have entered the bar manager's office. I knew what my manager would say by the word, but that did not bother me; I have decided to stand behind my opinion. After entering the bar office, I have noticed two familiar faces. They were silent, and both looked scared to make eye contact with me. I did the opposite by looking at their eyes straight, ready to shoot justice anytime.

Politely and firmly, I decided first to open up the conversation: "Any problems here, folks? I have a job to do if you are going to stay silent all day?"

Rashid was putting his thumb finger under his dirty, arrogant chin. I have decided to surprise him a little more, so I made a few more steps towards him.

"Did you have to come to cry to the bar manager? You did not dare to deal with me on your own?" I could not help it with my direct question. He kept quiet.

"John, you cannot talk to my assistant like that. He is your supervisor, and you need to respect him, regardless of your opinion!"

I answered promptly: "Sir, with all respect, let me tell you something: Our respect is earned, not given. You have to side up this arrogant, untrained assistant manager who mistaken his job description onboard the ship; I completely understand that. But let me also remind you of one thing, "Management role on the ship is mainly to inspire and motivate crew members, not to make them feel more stressful and anxious about doing their job". That's exactly what happened earlier at the Aft bar."

Assistant manager Rashid was still surprisingly quiet; he probably still gathered the courage to say something. Finally, he mumbled something unclear, without even making eye contact. "John, I don't know why you needed to respond to me in that manner earlier; I was doing my job," Rashid said.

"No, dude, you were not doing your job; that is the main problem here. If you treat people in my bar like slaves, certainly that won't happen, I can assure you. Your uniform does not make you earn our respect; it's your actions towards the crew that should be the first inevitable lesson of ethically sustainable leadership onboard the cruise ship."

I was not sure if he understood my point. Emil looked up at me and said, "I will not give you a written warning today; because of your high ratings in customer service, we all know how you perform at your job, and therefore you will be given one more chance," he concluded his point.

"Regardless of the circumstances, I always stand by good values. Yet, I will also strongly stand against bad values. It's your call, Rashid!" I left the bar office with a strong statement.

Chapter 14
Legacy

During that contract, that was just one of the many times I have persistently pursued justice on board the ship while personally not being concerned about any possible circumstances. Why would I be? Because of my job security is on the line? Money? Those reasons were simply not good enough. My basic priority was always to fight for the rights of the thousands of crew members on board who were scared to speak up for themselves.

Besides that, the foundation of my job security was already solid. I was repeatedly nominated for the month award's best employee, and that did not come from my managers. It came from the thousands of satisfied guests onboard who wrote down my name in their customer feedback forms after their cruise was finished. Those guests did not have a clue that while I was providing them with the best possible customer service, at the same time, I was fighting a massive battle with a slavery management regime on board, not for myself, but the thousands of other crew members. I climbed a rough, steep, dark, dangerous, undiscovered and unknown mountain.

Without a doubt, I did not accept to become part of that slavery regime. Therefore, those untrained managers lacking pure human qualities, compassion, empathy, and effective leadership were scared of the change I was persistently proposing on board. They could not understand that I was ready to go alone against the rotten values and poor management onboard the cruise ship. Yet, for that reason, I became their high priority target; I knew that. They were constantly looking for my mistake. They kept together like a bunch of hyenas, looking for the chance to set me up and to get rid of me, once and for all. But instead of stepping back, I was like a pit bull who would bite a tire and automatically lock his jaw on it and never let it go. Unfortunately for them, I was focused on paying attention to the details. My name kept coming up in customer service feedback forms; it was directly forwarded in the cruise line headquarters, which was a solid and thick concrete foundation for my job security. In other words, my working performance was significantly increasing company ratings. That gave me confidence, and I used that hard-earned reputation on board to pursue my dream of creating a fair, sustainable working environment.

There were days when I felt weak and tired. But you can never show to the hyenas your weakness. Does the brave lion run away when 20 hyenas are chasing him down? No, he stands up for his values and fights for his freedom and glory. He might be outnumbered, but his fighting spirit will always prevail.

If we all perform well only when we feel good, we probably will not accomplish much. When I did not feel like acting, I adjusted my plan. Instead of feeling to act, I would act myself into feeling. In other words, even if I was feeling exhausted and drained, I kept smiling and never stopped my fight for good values onboard the cruise ship. There was pure, the ultimate goal – creating a lasting, fundamental change in the management system onboard the cruise ships, setting the sail to the new, better world.

Diamonds never crack under pressure

Legacy is what we were created for; I always believed so – something that will make a beneficial impact on the world around us, long-lasting difference. Cruise ship taught me about the inevitable price that has to be paid on the way to our legacy fulfilment: bigger the goals, more significant the obstacles. Requesting permission to radically change the entire management style on board was the same as going into the cage with 100 hungry hyenas.

Anyway, I always liked the lions more than hyenas. Both animals are predators, but lion strength comes together with their glorious roar and determination to win every battle.

My roar for seaman's justice was just a warning that hungry hyenas are coming. Lions could sometimes be outnumbered, but they would never step back, no matter how many hungry hyenas are coming.

It was not easy to stay focused and to remain disciplined for many months at sea. What kept my desire solid was the ability to perform under pressure.

The difference between stone and diamond is not significant. They belong to the rock's family. What sets the huge difference is how they react when being exposed to the pressure. Stone easily cracks under pressure, and the diamond does exactly the opposite-it shines even more under pressure.

The cruise ship environment was the same. We were continuously looking for a way to shine under tremendous pressure, despite any circumstances. Here is one story about the incredible performance under pressure from my military days before joining the cruise ship.

Military discipline

There is no such thing as perfection in life. Moments when everything will settle down in perfect order, that scenario simply does not exist. Can we wait for those ideal moments when we would feel well-rested, in a good mood, eager, fresh, and energised to only then chase down our goals and fulfil our most incredible dreams? If we depend on our mood changes and temporary feelings, if we delay action while waiting for some better days to come, an ideal moment for that will never arrive. That moment, even if it arrives, it will last only for a short period, and we could not rely on it permanently. We all experience external factors every day, definitely we cannot control that, but our determination to overcome any obstacle along the way – indeed, we can.

During my military days, I have learned a lot. Food, water, proper sleep, a warm meal, water for taking a shower, soap, clean, ironed clothes, soft mattress, and spacious bad, those were the things that before my military service I often took for granted. Before I served in the military, I never paid attention to those things that I considered normal, automatically given to us.

In one of the most brutal military training centres globally, I used to sleep only two hours every night, had on average just one meal per day, and took a shower only once a month. At that time, military commanders were building our physical and mental resilience.

From a different perspective, I appreciate those thighs much more. I often look at the food on my table with a large amount of respect. During my military days, I was forced to move my limitations to the next level to survive the harsh living environment. Being a part of the sniper team, I have quickly learned that getting out of our comfort zone is the first and most essential step towards personal growth.

I remember one cold, windy night while I was in military service. The rain was consistent throughout the night; it was around 3 am, just when we finally got a chance to take a few hours of sleep after several days without it.

Suddenly, the prominent commander stormed into our sleeping room, and with his rough, loud voice, he screamed, "Soldiers! All of you lazy bugs, you have five minutes to get out of your warm beds and position yourselves in front of the training centre, with complete uniform and all your weapons."

I did not have much time to think about what was happening. I quickly dressed up and took my AK47, three knives, two bombs, gas masks, and first aid equipment. While only half awaken, I have managed to drag myself into the instructed position in front of the military object. It was 20 of us who lined up quickly and neatly in an organised order. Worn out, tired soldiers were standing frozen in the heavy rain and exposed to the strong winds.

While the rain was getting harder, a powerful voice suddenly tore the silence like thunder.

"Soldiers, you are the special kind. You made it on time here; it took you five minutes to organise yourself and get in your position. Impressive work. I know that you did not expect this exercise, especially at this time of the night, but that is the purpose of this training; you need to be ready at any given time. There is no single minute to remain in your comfort zone. In 30 minutes from now, we are conducting a night-time shooting exercise. We will push your limits to the next level," he concluded in his passionate speech.

Tired, hungry, and wet from the rain, battered by the strong winds lashing our faces, I started to move slowly together with my squad; we marched towards the nearby military training field.

This powerful military drill was divided into five different stages of night shooting.

Target was set at 20 m, 40 m, 60 m, 80 m, and 100 m. Improvised targets were coming unexpectedly, one by one, followed by some strange, disturbing sounds. The goal of this drill was to present our ability to perform under pressure.

Finally, my turn came up, and without significant problems, I have successfully shot the first four targets. The last target was the most complicated one. I had to put my gas mask on through the very low visibility. Thick smoke was intentionally created just in front of me. I could not breathe properly, and I had a terrible headache. I was hungry, sleepy, thirsty, overtired.

In these kinds of circumstances, it wasn't easy to focus. Yet, patiently, I was waiting for my target to come up. I was ready to pull the trigger at any needed time. Usually, it would take only a few seconds before the next target comes up, but nothing happened this time. Five minutes passed, way too long; it seemed like an eternity, ten minutes gone, still nothing.

Suddenly, while waiting for my target to come up, I have realised the key to this brutal military exercise is self-discipline and patience.

Finally, after 14 minutes of waiting, my target came up. On my right-hand side, with lightning speed, an improvised picture of the terrorist came up. That was my only chance. Like a blink of my eye, now or never. It was too dark, foggy, rainy, and windy. The moment of the truth has arrived; I was thinking. My face was full of mud and rain. Painful blisters on the feet were keeping me awake. I knew that I had to remain focused and wisely use only one remaining bullet. Despite how I felt at that moment, I needed to stay calm under pressure. I kept my breath for a second to avoid the AK47 movement.

Slowly and calmly, I have finally pulled the trigger in perfect momentum.

The next thing was a loud noise from the officers around me. Of all drill participants on that rainy and cold night, I was the only one who managed to shoot all five targets successfully.

It was that dark and stormy night that taught me a powerful life lesson. There is no perfect moment for us to shoot. When we have a sudden opportunity, we need to remain calm and give our best shoot despite all the difficult circumstances around us.

Inspired to survive

After five months onboard the ship, my working schedule constantly changed from week to week. Management was probably trying to test my resilience by adjusting my working areas. They kept moving me around the ship bars: Casino bar, Lobby Bar, Pool bar, Aft bar, Crew bar. Despite intense and endless working hours, I have found a way to sustain my focus and preserve my energy. The module of behaviour that was my survival strategy set me apart from other crew members. No matter what adversity I was facing, I remained focused and highly professional towards my guests.

One day, while I was checking the notice board in the bar office, I saw the new Leadership Development Program for all departments onboard the ship. The company has stolen my ideas and my original work without even letting me know and they decided to implement that, without my involvement. At that moment, I have realised that I came upfront with my vision; with no hesitation, I landed all my prospects and research, and the company took it away.

However, one part of me still felt accomplished because my idea was good. On the other hand, the company took my materials without my approval, which bothered me a lot from the inside.

Yet, it fuelled the flame in my spirit at the same time. I felt betrayed and used for company purposes. My presence on board became a quick spark in the infinity of the universe. Suddenly, that shiny spark was extinguished by greedy company ambition. Those were the office people who wanted fame for being an innovator, who implemented and executed my own idea fleet-wide.

The cruise line gave strict orders for the untrained, biased management onboard. Any spark of creativity representing some danger for their cruel systems onboard the ship was meant to be extinguished immediately. In my case, the only difference was that my idea was recognised and taken on board, but the office people who stole it away realised that they could certainly benefit from it.

Some of the cruise ship managers appeared to know about what was happening. The hotel director, who would usually not talk to me for a long time, stopped me one day while passing through the crew corridor.

Surprisingly, he asked me, "John, I heard that you gave the senior officers shoreside some idea. Is that true?"

"It is true, sir. In the past ten years, my dream was to create a sustainable, lasting change for the ship's working environment. Change is inevitable; I believe so. Therefore, I was happy to contact office people and present my management change idea. Excitingly, I gave them all my materials and knowledge; this company is already part of me; that was my strongest motivation." Passionately I had tried to explain my Leadership Development Program.

"Yes, John, I do understand your point of view, and I can see that you have a lot of potentials; all I am saying is friendly advice that maybe you should not give away all your materials and ideas just like that," the hotel director replied straight forward.

"It's okay sir, I am not asking anything in return. Only chance to be part of the team who will execute and implement this program onboard the ships fleet wide." I was trying to justify my actions.

"Well, good luck with everything John. You might need it…" the hotel director concluded his thought and kept walking fast towards his office.

At that moment, everything became crystal clear to me. The company was happy to take my idea on board; they took it away as a valued asset for improving working operations. I was just a number with no existence; my effort was not validated or recognised. They did not care about time, energy, dedication, and sleepless nights. The product and recipe for their promotion were there.

In the next couple of weeks on board, I have heard that the Leadership Development Program has been widely implemented fleet-wide, all management departments were taking part in it.

Somehow, inner satisfaction still existed in my feelings. A considerable change was set to occur because of that idea that was already validating itself.

Chapter 15
Electrical Shock

At the end of my fifth month on board, something happened, which proved to be a life-changing experience.

One morning, I woke up ready for a regular day at work. The ship was docked in San Juan, Puerto Rico. Our ship vocabulary was what we called my 'day off'.

That was not the actual day off; the only difference between the sea day and port days was that I started a little bit late in San Juan at 3pm.

When the ship arrives in the port, sometimes we can go outside for a short stroll. But at that time, in the port of beautiful San Juan, I needed to do my laundry in the morning, and during afternoon hours just before my work, we had some mandatory safety drill. At 3pm exactly, I showed up at my work at the bustling bar on Deck 10. At that moment, I did not know that what was about to happen would change my life forever.

Apart from our beverage service, long cocktail list, beers, and wines, we made complimentary popcorn for our guests in the bar. As a routine technical part of my job, I plugged the cable into a nearby socket. While ensuring that everything is ready for popcorn, I have cautiously turned on the popcorn machine.

Suddenly, I have got an electrical shock. From the impact itself, I was grounded. Being half awake, I saw my colleagues helping me get down to the medical centre. When we came downstairs on deck 0 in front of the infirmary, it was already evening and closed. The nurse on duty gave me something for the pain, and they sent me to go on my break shortly after the incident.

I have sustained severe injuries, but I was treated very poorly by the medical team and management onboard the ship despite that.

Management onboard the ship has intentionally tried to cover up that incident and remove their responsibility because they were aware that they put my life in danger by letting me operate an unsafe popcorn machine. The old, overused, cracked cable was lying on the popcorn machine's metal cabinet, and when I have tried to open that cabinet, I was struck by electricity. For a few seconds, I could not remove my arm from the popcorn machine from the electricity impact itself. Shortly after the incident occurred, my supervisor told me that he would take care of all the paperwork about the incident, all hazard incident reports, and everything else.

At that moment, I felt chest pain and pain in my right arm. On that very same evening, after taking just a short break, I was told to go back to work and 'be careful this time' while also being given some pain medication for my right hand.

On that same evening, we were told by our supervisor and electrician to continuously operate that popcorn machine and put some paper bags under the broken cable while still making popcorn to avoid further electricity shock. The damaged and cracked wire of the popcorn machine was replaced only on the next day.

For the next two weeks, I kept working while drinking many pain relievers every day despite everything. About two weeks after the incident, I went to the medical centre once again because I was still having pain in my arm, and for the first time in my life, I have developed hypertension. Every day I had constant chest pain and dizziness. My blood pressure was extremely high at that time. I was told by the ship physician that I had developed the medical condition of hypertension. Despite drinking my medication, my blood pressure was still high, and the doctor still kept me for another day off duty. I have also notified the doctor that I still have pain in my right hand and chest, but he prescribed me a stronger pain killer.

A couple of days later, I followed up with the doctor in the ship medical centre. My condition improved after taking many medications, and I was sent back to work.

The next day, from my colleagues, I have found out that there was no single email, report or note about that particular incident that happened to me, even though my managers were very well aware of what happened. They were probably trying to do a cover-up and remove their responsibility for this entire event.

For that reason, I went to the HR manager and brought a copy of the Work Order placed for the cracked popcorn machine wire to be replaced, and I asked the HR manager why there was no single email or report about the incident. It seemed like repairing the popcorn machine was much more important than taking care of its employees' health.

The HR manager ordered a formal investigation, and the bar manager and chief security were instructed to finally make a new crew injury report, which was amazingly missing. The security officer made a video of the popcorn machine, and they finally completed an investigation with all signatures and details about the incident being written down. Copy of that crew injury report incident was given to me only days later, just because I was very persistent.

I went to the medical centre for a follow-up, and the doctor told me that the pain in my arm would certainly go away in a few weeks; he said that it was only a muscle contraction and nothing to worry about. The medical staff on board insisted that everything was wonderful, and they sent me back to work once again. They also gave me the BP checklist and told me to come back to the medical centre to check on my BP every time.

The next day, I came back to check my BP and the result was 200/120, but the nurse wrote in my checklist 151/82. When I asked him why he wrote different numbers, he said, "You are working now; that's why you are here on the ship; it's better like this for all of us."

So I was rushed back to work.

About three weeks after the incident, my condition got worst. I felt very dizzy and had robust chest pain. I felt terrible migraine and vibration in the left side of my neck. I called my manager, and they sent me urgently to the medical centre.

The infirmary was closed at that time, but they took me inside as an emergency case. Blood pressure was 200/120 at one point, my heartbeat was 120, and my level of Calcium was critically low. The doctor decided to give me a two-hour potassium infusion, and they checked on my BP every five minutes. I was given medication for lowering my BP and also Loranzempan. That night, the doctor told me that they might leave me in the hospital shoreside upon arrival in the port of Amber Cove because I had got Hypokalemia. As per what doctor said, I could easily have kidney failure, stroke, heart attack, or permanent blindness that night. He was undecided either to send me to the hospital on the land the following day or not.

Around 01:00 am, after the infusion was completed, my blood pressure was still high 170/110, despite being infused with a lot of medication. Undecided about what to do next, medical staff members sent me back to my cabin and told me to come back in the morning. When I came to see the doctor the following day, my condition was still bad. I have asked the doctor to make a shoreside appointment because I wanted to see the cardiologist, neurologist, and orthopaedic specialist.

The ship was docked in the US port, St Thomas.

The doctor told me they could send me to see the specialist shoreside only the next week in Cozumel, Mexico; he added that Cozumel's specialist is the 'trusted company doctor'.

I did not clearly understand that part because before that scheduled arrival in Cozumel, Mexico; the ship would be docked in three Us ports: St Thomas, San Juan, and Port Canaveral. It seemed that they did not want me to go to the neutral, third-party medical institution in the US because I could present to the valid shoreside specialist with all irregularities when it comes to terrible and inadequate medical treatment onboard the ship.

However, the following days, I was still unfit for duty and kept on my medical off status.

Being isolated in my small, dark cabin, without sunlight, with considerable management pressure, without any therapy besides the trial-and-error medication provided daily by the medical team on board, my condition worsened.

I was told by doctors on board that I can't stay on the vessel longer than seven days without work. They agreed that my medical condition was complicated. At the same time, 'by the company procedure' I can't be sent home on the medical sign off the ground.

Instead, I was sent to the HR manager. She told me that I have two options – either I can *resign if I want* or take an emergency leave and pay for my ticket and all medical expenses home.

That was simply insane, a level of disrespect, and such a ridiculous statement from someone whose job is to be a Human Resource manager. At that moment, I was still unfit for duty, without the option to see the shoreside specialist. Still, at the same time, I could not stay on board for more than seven days without working, and that's why HR offered me to *resign*, saying that my condition is not bad enough to go home on medical sign-off status.

Well, that's what they gave me after ten years of hard work, after being an employee of the month several times in my career, just because I have developed severe medical conditions while doing my job.

I have asked the HR manager if I should wait until I get a heart attack, stroke or kidney failure to be sent home on medical sign-off status. At that moment, I felt like a thrown, overused pair of socks, ready to be replaced by the company's cruelty regime. That afternoon, at the end of the very stressful conversation with HR director, I was forced to go home on

'Emergency leave' and pay for all my flight tickets and medical expenses.

For sure, that was against Seaman Working Rights. The first employee in the cruise ship industry was probably sent home on 'Emergency leave' after being medical off for seven straight days before getting off the ship.

One day before going home, I went to speak with Staff Capitan. After explaining my situation to him, he was baffled and shocked to hear that company forced me to take an 'Emergency leave'. He told me that, unfortunately, he couldn't change that because he is not the one deciding about those things and can't make any adjustments regarding my case.

Forced sign-off leading to a struggle

Frustrated, injured, sick, stressed, and on the edge of a mental breakdown the following day, I left the ship. After arriving home, I stayed in the hospital and paid for all medical checkups with doctors, cardiologists, professors of psychiatry, neurologists, orthopaedics.

The conclusion was given by a team of specialists that I have developed several symptoms caused by electrical shock. They told me that I would have maintenance medication for the rest of my life. The psychiatry professor also diagnosed that I have a permanent post-traumatic disorder and that the recovery process will be long, slow, and uncertain. The orthopaedic assessed my arm injury. I had a terrible arm injury that will take a long time to recover, and future surgery will be required. After an MRI was conducted, the doctor wrote his statement; I was sent for several months on physical therapy, Plasma Thrombocyte injection in my arm. At the end, I have had a complicated surgery on my arm that was performed in my hometown. The government-appointed court professor of psychiatry wrote my diagnose about permanent damage to my mental health.

The mandatory medical records that I had gotten just before joining the ship about eight months before injury showed that my health was excellent before signing on that ship.

After being forced to leave the ship in a very inhuman circumstance, my life drastically changed. The company distanced from my case and replaced me in a matter of minutes, just like I never existed before.

Honestly, that was a tough time for my family and me.

After being a role model for the company for ten years, I did not deserve to be left out like this. I have served that company with honour, pride the best I could. In my ten years of working experience, I have consistently shown care and respect towards colleagues and guests. I wanted to believe that I was part of the team, and for that, I dedicated the best years of my life to the cruise line company.

Since the injury onboard the ship, everything has changed. They were more concerned about washing away company responsibility from my injury incident instead of sincerely helping me in my complicated recovery process.

Because for them, I was just one more number without identity and meaning. When I tried to reach out by phone to the head office to express my concerns, they did not let me finish my sentence while introducing myself politely. Instead, the voice on the phone repeatedly said, "What is your crew ID number?"

It was no surprise at all; I don't have a name for them, just a number. The company felt comfortable and protected despite everything that happened because all of their ships were purposely registered in Panama to get away from any Seaman Rights responsibility. They probably believe that they can buy anything or anyone with all of their money, including myself. And yet, cruise ship companies can get away most of the time because there is a lot of hidden pain from many crew members worldwide on a day-to-day basis.

I was probably one of the many crew members who was forced to take an emergency leave or resign straight after being medical off.

Being given an option to quit after that happened was unbelievable, surreal, beyond any prediction. After all these years of commitment, service, and dedication, this is what I have got from them.

Summary

No names, just a number.

Today, three years after I was forced to leave the ship on emergency status, I have to look for a few dollars to support my family. I took a loan from the bank to pay off that expensive medical recovery treatment, and now I am still unable to provide an everyday life for my family. I have got a complicated arm surgery in attempt to save the punctuality of my right arm.

After all, the cruise line company does not care; I am just one more number for them. They are too busy building their new ships while my family is suffering and praying for justice. Company profits are the highest priority. Targets are there to be achieved; everything else, including human life on board the ship, is not important at all. Instead, crew members are just temporary numbers that are yet to be squeezed and used until the last drop of their sweat.

Thank you from the bottom of my heart for all of my guests from the cruise ships worldwide, lovely and unique people. 90 percent of all of the guests I have ever met on board the ships were simply great folks, gorgeous people. With predominantly stormy and unfair conditions behind the crew members' life on board, you made a huge positive difference for all of us. It is something that significantly helped all our families back home and it justified that lonely time spent at sea. With all appreciation of your tips, that was not the significant difference you created. More importantly, thank you for understanding, smiling back to us, patiently waiting for your turn to be served. Thank you to those who went further to make good comments about our job onboard the ship. Doing that made our jobs more secure and extraordinarily contributed to the cruise ship industry. Thank you for showing us compassion and empathy. Indeed, you have paid for those cruises, and you had all rights to be demanding and picky. Yet, you choose to show us an extraordinary level of respect, and therefore, you made our life on board much easier.

Because we are mainly surrounded by those biased, untrained, arrogant managers on board the ship, our amazing guests made a tremendous positive difference for us most of the time. Our guests made us feel validated for the hard work we do. That matters more than any amount of money in this world. As a crew member on board, our purpose and legacy are to create memorable, unforgettable memories for all our guests. When we do so, the feeling of inner fulfilment is overwhelming and astonishing.

For the minority of the guests onboard, chronically unhappy and constantly looking for things to complain about, please reconsider your options in the future. When you constantly look for a reason to complain, your life also becomes miserable before you are even aware of it. If you purposely complain about waiting for your food two minutes extra, delayed tender boat to get you offshore, too many people in the swimming pool, or some crew members simply did not remember your name, please pause for a second and think about it. The same rule will apply on the ships, on the land, everywhere you go.

Those hard-working people on board the ships are already trying their best to provide you with the best possible customer service. If you only show a little respect towards the crew members, it will bounce back to you like a boomerang. We will all appreciate your gesture, and believe me, kindness never goes unnoticed! It travels millions of miles!

Thank you all; great people!

References

Maxwell, J. C. (1993). *Developing the leader within you.* Nashville: T. Nelson.

Maxwell, J. C. (1990). *21 irrefutable laws of leadership* (2nd ed.). Thomas Nelson.

Covey, S. R. (1989). The seven habits of highly effective people: Restoring the character ethic.

New York: Simon and Schuster.

Bradberry, T., & Greaves, J. (2009). *Emotional Intelligence 2.0*. TalentSmart.

Covey, Stephen R. (2004). The 8th habit: from effectiveness to greatness. New York: Free Press.

Maxwell, J. C. (1999). *The 21 indispensable qualities of a leader: Becoming the person that people will want to follow*. T. Nelson.

Maxwell, J. C. (1960). The 5 levels of leadership. New York, NY: Centre Street.

Maxwell, J. C. (2009). *How successful people think: Change your thinking, change your life*.